MANAGEMENT SKILLS IN MARKETING

Stephen Morse

Amsterdam • Johannesburg • London
San Diego • Sydney • Toronto

Copyright © 1994 by Stephen Morse

First edition published in 1982 by McGraw-Hill Book Co. (UK) Ltd.

Pfeiffer & Company
8517 Production Avenue
San Diego, CA 92121-2280

Copyright under International, Pan American, and Universal Copyright Conventions. All rights reserved. No part of this book may be reproduced or transmitted in any form or by any means, electronic or mechanical, including photocopying, recording, or by any information storage-and-retrieval system, without written permission from the publisher. Brief passages (not to exceed 1,000 words) may be quoted for reviews.

This publication is designed to provide accurate and authoritative information in regard to the subject matter covered. It is sold with the understanding that the publisher is not engaged in rendering legal, accounting, or other professional service. If legal advice or other expert assistance is required, the services of a competent professional person should be sought. *From a Declaration of Principles jointly adopted by a Committee of the American Bar Association and a Committee of Publishers.*

Page Compositor: Sybil Ihrig, VersaTech Associates
Cover: Tom Lewis, Inc.

ISBN: 0-89384-252-4

Printed in the United States of America.

Printing 1 2 3 4 5 6 7 8 9 10

CONTENTS

Preface ix

Part I: Skills Involved in Planning Marketing 1

1. **Planning Marketing: The Marketing Manager's Input Into the Company Plan** 3
   The Company Purpose 3
   Key Areas 7
   Means of Measurement 8
   Constraints and Limitations 9
   A Cyclical Pattern 10
   Marketing Planning Schedule 13
   Obstacles 15
   Checklist of Skills and Action for Chapter 1 16

2. **Marketing Research and Marketing Information** 19
   Market Assessment 24
   Product Evaluation 26
   Marketing Information Systems 31
   Preliminary Investigation 32
   Identifying Problems 34
   Using an Information System 35
   Checklist of Skills and Action for Chapter 2 36

3. **At What Market Should We Aim?** 39
   Types of Segmentation 40
   Strategies for Segments 47
   Eliminating Wasted Effort 51
   Forecasting Sales 52
   Objectives 62
   Establishing Priorities—Pareto's Law 65

	Moving Annual Totals and Z Charts	66
	Checklist of Skills and Action for Chapter 3	68
4.	**Assessing the Ingredients of the Marketing Mix**	**71**
	The Four P's	72
	Sales/Cost Ratio	80
	Checklist of Action Points for Chapter 4	81

Part II: Skills Involved in Organizing Marketing 83

5.	**Marketing Organization**	**85**
	What Does Marketing Organization Involve?	85
	Organization Principles	90
	Types of Organization	91
	Relationships and Systems	94
	Marketing Activities and the Place of Sales Operations	96
	Checklist of Action Points for Chapter 5	99
6.	**Improving Management Performance**	**101**
	Starting Points	101
	Management Development	104
	The Manager's Needs	106
	Job Analysis	107
	Action Plans	112
	Review	112
	Benefits	113
7.	**The Skill of Managing Time**	**117**
	Time Use	117
	Time Log	119
	Time Analysis	122
8.	**Working in Groups**	**127**
	A Model	128
	Influences on Behavior in Groups	130

	Norms and Their Development	132
	Improving Efficiency	134
	Group Types	135
	Organizing the Group	136
	Summary	140
9.	**Managing Communications**	**143**
	What Should Be Communicated?	143
	How to Communicate	145
	Written Communication	147
	Making Presentations	154
	Communication Instruments	160
	Communication With Outside Contractors	162
	Inventory of Communication Tools	164

Part III: Skills Involved in Controlling Marketing — **171**

10.	**Marketing Manager's Profit Responsibilities**	**173**
	Financial Statements	173
	Marketing and Selling Costs and Contribution	178
	Primary Ratios of Turnover and Profit	180
	Costing and Pricing	184
	Budgets	187
11.	**Decision Making and Accounting**	**191**
	Cash-Flow Analysis and Measurement	191
	Project Evaluation	192
	Capital Investment in New Products	195
	Evaluating Investment	197
	Opportunity Cost	200
	Break-Even Charts, Profit-Volume Relationships, and Limiting Factors	202
12.	**Controlling Marketing Effectiveness**	**207**
	Limitations on Control Activities	208

Controllable Factors	209
Inherent Product Appeal	213
Marketing Cost Analysis	214
Establishing and Checking on Objectives	215
Activities and "Payoff"	217
Final Remarks	219
Checklist for Chapter 12	220
Appendix	**221**
References	221
Further Reading	222
Index	**223**

ACKNOWLEDGMENTS

I gratefully acknowledge permission from the following publishers to reproduce copyright material.

AMACOM for Tables 11.4 and 11.5. Reprinted by permission of the publisher, from *Financial Tools for Marketing Administration,* by L. Gayle Rayburn, © 1976 by AMACOM, a division of American Management Associations, pages 84 and 85. All rights reserved. National Industrial Conference Board for Table 1.4. Reprinted with permission from *Selected Examples of Marketing Planning Schedules,* Exhibit 9, pages 36 and 37.

Penguin Books Ltd for Figures 10.7 and 10.8. Reproduced by permission of the publisher, from *An Insight into Management Accounting,* by John Sizer (Penguin Education, Second edition, 1979) pages 192, 193 and 425, © John Sizer, 1969, 1975, 1977, 1978, 1979, and to Gerard Scholtes of Peat Marwick in the Hague for the diagrams on pages 175 and 180.

PREFACE

For a number of years I have been interested in the fact that management (and it is usually spelled with a capital M) seems to have ignored the need to develop skills. Thus a manager is expected to *know* how to manage; management training usually consists of instruction in principles and techniques. In fact, there must be many managers who, when first faced with the job, sit at their desk and wonder where to start. The boundaries that are drawn between principles and techniques, between deciding what to do and getting it done, are never very clear. But the crevasse between knowing what to do and being able to do it seems to me to be both wide and deep.

In many cases the new manager looks for a model—a previous "boss," his father, his schoolmaster—which he can use to help solve the problem. If his previous boss has solved a problem in an authoritarian fashion, then he will certainly start either by slavishly following or by totally rejecting the "model."

What this book attempts to do is not to try to replace the model with a totally different one, but to provide both the new and untried manager, and the manager who has been "just managing" for years with a sort of "crib," a short reference book that says something brief and, I hope, to the point about a number of subjects that are constantly facing managers. Because marketing managers have often arrived from other disciplines (I have known marketing managers who started life as engineers, accountants, sociologists, salesmen, economists, and electronic wizards) this book is about the skills exercised by marketing managers, even though many of them are used by managers in other parts of the business. The book is *not* about marketing techniques and strategies, which vary from firm to firm and are subject to the whims of fashion (for example, in the 1980s we seemed to be more interested in fighting competitors than in satisfying customers!). It *is* about the management skills required to achieve results.

Managers, whether of marketing or any other function in the business, are concerned not only with the creative and strategic decision making, but, more importantly, with getting things done. They need tools and techniques. They need an understanding of what techniques are available to get the plans to work and what controls are necessary to check that plans are achieving the desired result.

The development of the marketing concept and the need for marketing management are still, for many companies, recent phenomena. The need for the "marketing concept" arose from the increase in discrimination by customers and the recognition that only by understanding and fulfilling customer requirements could adequate profits be made. Marketing was charged with coordinating and planning the total effort of the enterprise toward the customer. The main purpose of "marketing" is to ensure that the efforts of separate parts of the company, such as research, manufacture, sales, advertising, finance, accounting and customer-related activities, such as market research, product development, selling, sales promotion, and aftersales service are working as closely together as possible.

Therefore, this book is divided into parts that relate to the three aspects of management skills:

- Part One is about planning, including information collection and establishing the type of strategy to be followed.
- Part Two is about organizing, including the setting of objectives and the defining of results to be

achieved, together with some of the personal skills (managing time, group work, and communicating) necessary to get things done.
- Part Three is about controlling, including the aspects of accounting and profit/volume relationships and the effectiveness of the different marketing factors.

Each chapter is almost self-contained, and the book may be approached as a set of essays or readings, the thread being that all of them concern marketing management. No attempt, however, is made to provide an indication of the latest or most up-to-date views or research on a subject. Much of the content is basic and unchanging; certainly there is little that is new. I have included at the end of most chapters a self-evaluation checklist—a short reminder of the skills that may need practice. Knowing *how* to do something is often only the starting point for being able to do it. Practice is required if success is to be achieved.

Skill is defined in the *OED* as "practical knowledge in combination with ability; a craft, an accomplishment." This book is about some skills that may be valuable to marketing managers.

In the first edition, I assumed that all managers were male. Rather than change all the "hes" into "he/shes," I have assumed that there are equal numbers of male and female managers (indeed, in many businesses females outnumber males in the marketing functions) — so I hope that the reader will not be upset to find managers addressed as "he."

I

Skills Involved in Planning Marketing

1

Planning Marketing: The Marketing Manager's Input Into the Company Plan

The Chinese have a saying: "If we know not whither we are going, the road we travel matters little." If company planning is about the road we travel, then a basic requirement is first to know where we are going. Before a company can begin to establish objectives, either long or short term, it needs to identify the company purpose. (This is also called the mission or goal—names that help to distinguish this aspect of the company from its motivation.) Nor is the company purpose adequately described as a single objective. Cato the elder, with fanatical single-mindedness, ended every speech with the phrase *Delenda est Carthago* ("Carthage must be destroyed"), an objective that was eventually achieved. But such a single objective can rarely describe the purpose of a company; and the objectives of a business—be it a large multinational corporation or a small family business—can never be that simple.

The Company Purpose

For all practical purposes, company planning can be seen as a process in which Step One is to define the company purpose. A great number of subsequent misunderstandings and errors can be avoided by making this a first step. Even when an organization is being changed or modified to give more encouragement to enterprise by establishing profit centers or business units, it is still necessary to define precisely the purpose of such profit centers or business units. The purpose of the business is established by being able to answer the following questions:

- What exactly is our business?
- What business are we in?
- What needs and preferences of customers are we providing or serving?

The questions are easy enough to answer, given a moment's thought: Our business is making a particular product, we are producing packaging material for that product, and we are providing transportation for the finished product. It is, however, also easy to go on from these answers into setting objectives that push us into doing the wrong things better: making more of a product of the wrong sort because it is cheaper, producing a more complex material because it makes a contribution to overhead, buying bigger transportation vehicles because the break-even load factor is lower.

Of course, this is a joint task of all the top managers in a company, where the customer is represented by the marketing specialist (be this marketing director, commercial director, sales and marketing manager, etc.).

Establishing the purpose of the business is crucial. It affects everything that is done afterward. Let's take a look at the purpose of a national airline, for example. Is it simply to provide transportation for the country's citizens, or for other people who want to come to a particular country for a vacation, or is it an organization that supports businesses that want to export or import a product or service? Is this airline's purpose to be a department of government, providing a service regardless of cost to locations where products or services are believed to be needed? By looking at the airline from the outside, it is clear that its customers are multinational and have a number of "wants"—but they are also the government as a major shareholder, and other stakeholders, its employees, for example. One could begin a statement of company purpose by saying: To provide employment to a certain number of people by providing an international transportation service and go on to define levels of service by referring to customers and to business.

To illustrate the effect that specifying the business's purpose has on the other aspects of the business's activities can be seen in defining the purpose of a school. Is it to provide the next generation of industrial workers or to help the children to lead happy lives or, more cynically, to provide hard-working mothers with much-needed rest or, even more cynically, to provide employment for those who cannot find productive employment elsewhere? Of course any school has elements of all those definitions, and, perhaps, more schools have thought through the consequences of their purposes than have many businesses. To help in defining the purpose of a business, it is useful to consider the purpose as a three-dimensional cube.

- The *needs* that the business serves (customers' needs for food, clothing or shelter, legal advice, health care, entertainment, etc.)
- The *characteristics* of the customers (male or female, single or married, etc.)
- The *technology* used, or the way in which the needs of customers with identified characteristics are met.

If the purpose is described in these terms, future development would be likely to be along one of the sides of this

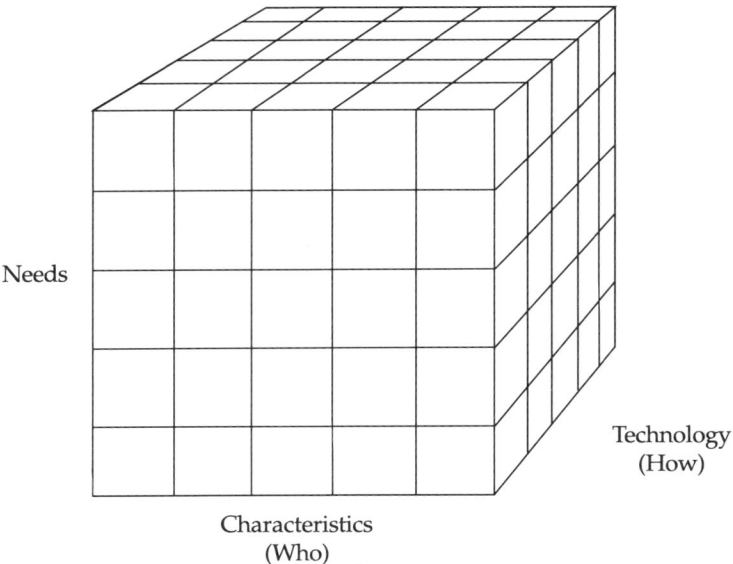

Figure 1.1 A Business Definition

three-dimensional cube; the business will provide satisfaction for the same needs in a wider marketplace, it will provide more services or products to the existing customer types, or it will develop different products or services using the same technology (see Figure 1.1).

The purpose defines what the enterprise sets out to do, and it also defines what it will not do. In *Up the Organization* author Robert Townsend described how Avis decided that it was "in the business of renting and leasing vehicles without drivers." This definition, says Townsend, kept Avis away from such diversions as the acquisition of motels, hotels, airlines, or travel agencies, which seemed to be related businesses, and thus very attractive in a period when growth by acquisition was popular.[1]

A company that manufactured chemicals for flavors and fragrances was very much tempted by the apparent size of the market of fragrances in soaps and detergents.

Having thought through the company's purpose, the company decided that fragrances developed for Parisian perfumery houses could only with tremendous difficulty coexist with scents used to disguise the homely smell of detergents. Thus temptation was resisted.

Key Areas

However, in this instance, more than a little help was received from Step Two and beyond. Step Two is a simple aid to planning. Because most businesses are very difficult to comprehend all at one time, it is helpful to break each step down into those areas where performance and results directly and vitally affect survival and prosperity. The temptation here is to look at the natural divisions of the enterprise, such as production, selling, accounting, personnel and so on. In *The Practice of Management* (which is still one of the best guides for the practicing manager), Peter Drucker suggests that there are eight key areas in any enterprise where excellence is vital.[2]

The reason for taking this step is to create a filing system or a sorting code that allows all the remaining steps of the planning process to be neatly docketed and ticketed.

The eight key areas are

1. Market standing.
2. Innovation.
3. Productivity.
4. The use of physical and financial resources.
5. Profitability.
6. Manager performance and development.
7. Performance and attitude of nonmanagerial staff.
8. Public responsibility.

Table 1.1 Ansoff's Matrix

	Products	
Markets	*Existing*	*New*
Present	Current business	Product development
New	Market development	Diversification

Many companies find they have other areas, either to include or to replace for these eight. In the 1990s, with the emphasis on Total Quality Management, it is probable that quality as a key area will appear on the list. If it is added, it will need to be carefully defined. Some businesses might add stock control or purchasing as key areas in their own right.

Naturally the one nearest and dearest to the marketing manager's heart is going to be market standing, since it comprises most of those aspects of the enterprise's operations for which the manager has responsibility and knowledge, such as the situation in each quadrant of Ansoff's matrix[3] (shown in Table 1.1), together with more detailed considerations of product strategy, distribution and pricing, and after-sales service.

The skill involved here is in reducing the number of "files" to a minimum, so as to make the analysis spare and rigorous. Some of those who have devised more elaborate company planning systems refer to these key areas as the economic factors essential to the success of a business.

Means of Measurement

Whatever your company calls them, means of measurement are important to success in your chosen business (or product/market area). More importantly, there needs to be means of measurement for each of the key areas, so that it is possible to assess what is happening; to chart progress toward results. This is Step Three, and finding these means is easier for some key areas than for others. Indeed, economists and statisticians are always seeking better ways of measuring the health of companies, and each measuring technique has a value when looking for a particular feature.

Each key area demands some means of measuring progress. For example, market standing might be measured by changes in market share, by profit or volume growth rates, or where the product (or service) is in its life cycle; innovation could be measured by the number of successful new products launched, or by expenditure on R&D; use of physical and financial resources would probably be measured by return on investment (ROI) or by profit after tax.

It is much more difficult to develop means of measuring the company image or the development of managers. The former can be done by regular effective study of the market; the latter by appraisal of progress and results. The important thing is to select a meaningful measuring unit and keep it over a period of years.

Constraints and Limitations

Step Four in building the foundation of the company's plan is the identification of the limits of discretion. It has been said that there is no freedom without laws. In establishing a planning framework there are a number of limitations and constraints that businesses define based on ethical or political standards: what level of quality is acceptable, what profit is reasonable, and how far to go to obtain it. There are also the constraints that society places, legally or morally—not only in the marketplace but also in the comptroller's office and the employment office.

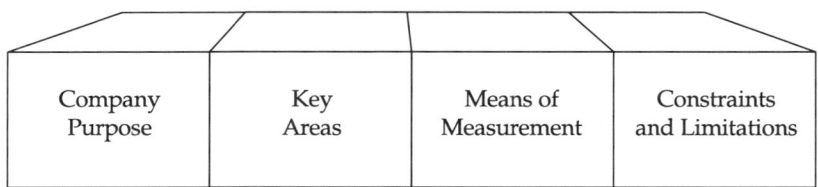

Figure 1.2   Building Blocks of the Company Plan

There will be a number of limitations and constraints in each key area, and these must be made explicit, so there are no surprises when the time comes to establish objectives.

A Cyclical Pattern

With these matters worked out there is now a framework on which to apply a cyclical planning process. The building blocks are shown in Figure 1.2.

With this framework, the company's top management team should now be able to move forward in the direction of setting objectives in the key areas that are vital to the performance and profitability of the business. The process is intellectually challenging; it requires a clear head and a willingness to set aside prejudices in advance.

In the business environment of today, objectives should focus on those critical factors on which the future of the business depends. This means that an analysis of strengths and weaknesses needs to be made, not just generally ("Let's sit down today and take a look at our strengths and weaknesses") but specifically and rigorously, examining each key area in turn.

The idea is to take each key area one at a time, listing everything about that key area that you think is important. By eliminating overlapping and repeating ideas and issues that might not seem important at present (they may be important in the future) a list of strengths and weaknesses that apply internally and can be immediately developed. The temptation is to put down every weakness and then search for a few strengths. One company listed its strengths and weaknesses as the positive and negative aspects of a particular subject: For example, under training and development of staff as a key area were listed

> Positive: Product knowledge of the sales force is good.
> Negative: No defined training program.
> Positive: Good salary levels.
> Negative: Commission system does not work.

Often a valuable first step is to draw up a checklist against which to evaluate strengths and weaknesses: For the key area market standing the questions in Table 1.2 could be a starting point. Checklists should always be thought-starters, not thought-inhibitors. They should contain, for the most part, open-ended questions, they should not be too long, and they should be immediately thrown out when the answers are automatic, unimportant, or boring.

While working groups within the company are collecting facts and figures to assess strengths and weaknesses, the chief marketing executive is the leading figure in the analysis of opportunities and threats—a look outside the company and an attempt to gauge the future—so that the question can be asked: Can our company build on its present strengths to take advantage of opportunities? In one company, the argument ran as follows: We have the strengths of an experienced and competent chief executive—but will it constitute a threat in the future (that he has no successor) or an opportunity (that he will not retire for five years)?

This analysis must take into account the political, social, economic, and technological influences on the company's

Table 1.2 Market Standing: Checklist of Questions

1. Is our market increasing or decreasing?
2. At what rate is it increasing or decreasing per year? Compared with the external environment (e.g., GNP)?
3. What is our share of the market? (Bear in mind the need to be very clear about market definitions.)
4. What are the important attributes of the product in terms of
   - Production?
   - Advertising?
   - The buyer?
   - The user?
5. Who makes the buying decision?
6. Do we depend on a few specific customers?
7. What are the strengths and weaknesses of our primary competitors?
8. Where is the product bought (distribution system)?
9. How logical is our product range?
10. What is the price structure?
11. How effective is our sales organization in terms of
    - Territories.
    - Order value.
    - Cost per product.
    - Cost per area.
    - Success ratios.
12. Where are our products in their life cycle?
13. Are new products under development?

present and potential customers—the factors most likely to affect the company's future. In larger companies, collecting this information may be the responsibility of a company planning section or a corporate economist, as shown in the example of integrating the marketing plan into the company planning process. (See the section called Marketing Planning Schedule, Table 4.1.) The example, incidentally, gives a clear insight into the ways in which marketing has a responsibility for the initial input into the company plan—such as field forecasts, marketing planning review, and marketing analysis for the five-year plan.

Marketing Planning Schedule

This section provides an overview for devising marketing plans. It shows

- The responsibilities of both marketing and sales personnel in developing annual marketing plans.
- The integration of marketing plans into the annual profit plan and five-year plan development process.
- The timetable of activities.

In the coming chapters some of the ways in which basic market information may be collected, collated, and distributed are discussed, which can lead to a perceptive analysis of current trends in the market and the color of the company's plan.

But the chief marketing executive has a dual role. A great deal of skill is called for, not only in trying to persuade the more down-to-earth managers to look around to see how far they have gotten and where they need to go, but also to make a diagnosis of the detailed results of marketing activities so as to derive objectives for individual functions within marketing: market research, product management, sales force, sales/order office, advertising and sales promotion, physical distribution, marketing services (such as forecasting and pricing), aftersales service, and ancillary services such as sales training.

To undertake such a dual role successfully there needs to be a clear understanding of organizational responsibilities and a clear program showing dates and time. The example given in Table 1.3 shows this very clearly, demonstrating perhaps that everything takes longer than anyone thinks, but

Table 1.3 Schedule for Annual Marketing Planning: A Diversified Manufacturer

Date	Activity	Participants
9/1	*Five-year economic forecast* A broad forecast based on projections of national economic growth, including forecasts of growth in major end-use markets for company products.	Corporate economist
9/10	*Field forecasts* Forecasts of industrial materials and contract and supply departments sales by products.	Zone managers Regional managers
9/20	*Marketing planning review* Review of progress on current-year plans and outline of principal elements of next year's plans.	Director of marketing Marketing managers
9/30	*Market reearch annual forecast* Forecast based on economic forecast and opinions of marketing and sales managers.	Market research
10/10	*Five-year market growth and division penetration* Marketing analysis for the five-year plan.	Director of planning Director of marketing Director, commercial R&D
10/15	*Marketing and sales opinions of field forecasts*	Marketing managers Sales managers
10/20	*Preliminary annual and five-year plans* Factory five-year plan Factory annual plan Divisional administrative expense Five-year sales objectives	Division vice president VP—manufacturing Director of planning Director of marketing VP—general sales VP—special industry sales
11/10	*Preliminary review of annual and five-year profit plans*	Division vice president
11/20	*Annual marketing plans completed* Includes review with sales managers.	Director of marketing Marketing managers
11/25 – 12/15	*Revision and review* Annual and five-year plans • Sales • Manufacturing • Divisional expense	Division vice president VP—general sales VP—contract and supply department VP—special industry sales Director of marketing
12/15	*Marketing plans typed* Dress rehearsal Annual and five-year plans	Marketing managers Division vice president
12/20	*Presidential review*	President
1/10	*Marketing plans book issued* Includes budgets, policy objectives, marketing plans.	Director of marketing

that deadlines are essential if results are to be achieved on time (a necessary skill that all marketing managers must cultivate).

Obstacles

There are four major obstacles that can frustrate the marketing manager in his attempt to influence the company's planning process. First, there is often a lack of commitment to forward thinking from the chief executive—he is so busy running the business (putting out fires) that he has little energy left to maintain the necessary planning discipline. Secondly, the planning may be done by a separate planner, who is cut off from the realities of the business. Third, perhaps no real analysis is undertaken and plans are subject to the add-ten-percent syndrome. This syndrome means that last year's objectives and strategies are carried forward with a simple addition of 10 percent to revenue expectations and cost budgets. (Incidentally, this add-10-percent syndrome has been the primary affliction attacked by zero-base budgeting, though this would appear to be a sledge-hammer-to-crack-a-nut approach.) Fourth, and unfortunately this is often encouraged by marketing people, the company proceeds on the basis of a few good ideas, which tend first to obscure and then to overwhelm well-grounded planning.

The first step in establishing an effective marketing operation is to educate the organization as to the value of the function to the organization's overall success. Marketing interfaces with many other functions, and marketing cannot achieve its goals if nonmarketing personnel do not understand these interfaces.

Checklist of Skills and Action for Chapter 1

1. Does your company/unit have a clear statement of purpose? If not, write one! Be sure to address needs, characteristics, and technology.
2. What are the key areas of your business?
3. Do you regularly examine strengths and weaknesses in key marketing-oriented areas? (These areas include market standing and innovation.)
4. Has assessment of the external environment for opportunities and threats been done recently, under the guidance of the chief marketing executive? What was the result?
5. What objectives are set for each key area? For what period? Are these translated for individual divisions or units?
6. Do the nonmarketing managers in the company appreciate each customer's requirements?
7. Is there a regular matching of the company's product against market needs?
8. Does your marketing plan contain the following chapters? It should.

   Chapter 1. Introduction and Summary

   Chapter 2. General Assessment of the Market
   - Past history
   - Present position
   - Future expectations

   Chapter 3. Market Segmentation
   - Size and growth
   - Share
   - Competitors
   - Problems and solutions

Chapter 4. Product Range
- Current range
- Analysis of strengths and weaknesses
- New products to be launched

Chapter 5. Objectives and Priorities

Chapter 6. Marketing Mix

Chapter 7. Program for the Year

Chapter 8. Budgets

Chapter 9. Control and Review Systems

2
MARKETING RESEARCH AND MARKETING INFORMATION

In Chapter 1 it was postulated that a major skill which the chief marketing executive should possess is that of providing input into the company plan. In order to do this, he needs to know about markets and customers. But in order to carry out the other aspects of his management task, he also needs an intelligence service that can regularly provide such information.

It is fashionable to talk about a product/market strategy, believing that the two are permanently linked. Although this idea is of value for some aspects of decision making, the basic information actually needs to be collected in separate files. It is important to think of a market as a grouping of customers.

The kind of information that is to be collected should be divided into two sections: market assessment and product evaluation. In general, market assessment is concerned with knowledge about actual and potential customers, such basic facts as

- Number.
- Location.
- Age, sex, and salary (for industrial customers include size, turnover, buying patterns, etc.).

- Channels of distribution by type and location.
- Trends and changes in the above information.

This information can be sorted into identifiable market segments (more about this later) and the purchasing power of such segments. There also needs to be a comprehensive and continuously updated file of information on the extent and type of competition. This would include competition in alternative or substitute product offers and in end user distribution channels. Backing this up should be information about existing sales and contribution (see Chapter 10) by customer, channel, and geographical area or market. Table 2.1 is a useful starting point for what the marketing manager should know of each operating market; Table 2.2 lists the knowledge necessary when new markets are attacked.

Table 2.1 Major Areas of Information

Country Features	Market Character
Geography	GNP
Climate	Income distribution
Population density	Scope of product use
Language	Size and growth (units)
Politics	Import
Economy	Export
Culture	Price levels
Customers	*Competition*
Potential customers	Number of competitors
Major projects	Direct or indirect
Customer's decision makers	Market shares of major competitors
Influencers of decisions	Market coverage
Organization and size of typical customer	Reputation
	Financial position
Reputation	Production capacity
Financial standing	International links
Size scatter*	Vertical links in the system

*Proportion of large, medium, and small users

Table 2.2 Technical Aspects: Necessary Knowledge When Approaching New Markets

Organization and Regulation of Trade	Importing	Marketing and Distribution	Legal	Finance
Trade associations	Licensing	Distribution channels	Patents	Banks
Wholesalers	Duties/quotas	Salesmen and agents	Trademarks	Available finance
Governmental requirements	Certificates needed	Profit margins	Local legal assistance	Payment terms
	Taxation	Advertising media	Product liability	Credit levels
	Currency	Exhibitions	Labeling, etc.	
	Profit repatriation	Language, etc.*		
	Transport costs	Internal shipping		
	Customs costs			

*Including cultural problems

Product evaluation, on the other hand, is concerned with having a regular supply of information on

- Sales per product line per market.
- Trends in sales and market share per product.
- Competitive products and shares.
- Prices and price structures.
- Qualities the product possesses. (How does the product compare with others in terms of features, price, service, and value? What is its image in the view of the potential and actual customer? What are the features and benefits of the product?)

This last area is one where it is difficult for many manufacturers or producers to be objective, which is not surprising.

If by any objective test your product is as good as your competitor's, but he has 40 percent market share and you have only 8 percent, the temptation is to blame the ignorance of the market or the customer in not recognizing the undoubted advantages of possessing or using your product. This does occur; as often in industrial goods and services as in the more common and well-known consumer goods market.

The skills to be exercised by the marketing manager consist not only of devising suitable checklists and lists of information that *should* be available, but in selecting that information where more details will help with decision making. It cannot be too strongly stressed that superfluous information is not only expensive, it is confusing. (There is a point where your mind is made up; you do *not* need any more facts.)

So before undertaking research to acquire the information shown on the checklists, three important questions should be asked.

The first is: *What will be done with the information obtained?* or perhaps more sharply expressed: Do we really need more information to make this new decision, or to continue with our existing pattern of activity? The distressing thing is that in many companies with expert market research departments, or companies who use expert outside research agencies, there is still a tendency to hide market research findings in a nearby desk drawer because the findings either agree with the manager's experience ("We know that already!") or they disagree ("That's nonsense!"). This is regrettable, but it can be avoided by trying to establish in advance the value of the information in the decision-making process, and considering worst-case scenarios ("What will happen if it totally changes our assumptions?").

The second question to be asked is: *How significant will the information presented be*? This question is less likely to be asked in surveys conducted on well-recognized areas in the consumer market, though there are sometimes considerable misdirections of emphasis.

For example, if out of a random sample of 1700 respondents it is noted that 650 are trade unionists, as this is the normal spread of trade unionists in the population, this result would be expected. If, however, a high percentage of that group (68 percent) has a particular view, it is less than reliable to express this as "the view of the majority of trade unionists in the country."

So it is not reliability of the information that should be questioned, but that of the interpretation. However, in less rigorously conducted surveys the reliability question is the one that concerns the quality of the information being sought. Too often opinions rather than facts are collected. Too often potential buyers are not actually put into buying situations, but are only asked what they *might* do in a situation. Too often questions are aimed at sensitive areas of human behavior, where respondents are unwilling to be truthful. (For example, do we honestly know why we prefer one brand of tissue to another? Are we sufficiently aware of our own emotions and drives to explain our apparently irrational behavior when it comes to brand loyalty?)

As a result, brand managers continue to worry about why their brand, which had demonstrated itself in a blind test to be as good as the major competitor, or which the laboratory insisted was superior to the competitor's in terms of quality, ingredients, workmanship, etc., mysteriously only managed to gain a $7\frac{1}{2}$ percent share of the market.

The third question—*How much will it cost?* is at the same time more subtle and more difficult to answer. You may decide to use the more sophisticated approach of employing a market research agency, or you can use the students from one a nationally recognized business school or from your state or community college; in each case, the costs will be very different. But the question is concerned less with the cost per interview, or the price paid to the agency, than it is to the cost of making decisions without adequate information, or the cost of not doing what the research indicates should be done. The costs of continuing on a certain course can be considerable—can, indeed, be disastrous. The skills involved here are those of identifying the costs involved and then putting them down on paper.

Market Assessment

There are a number of well-known methods of assessing markets, but it is often not recognized that they can actually be alternatives or complements. This situation depends on the circumstances. The first is desk research from published sources of information. In the last ten to fifteen years, the sources of information and availability have proliferated and improved. One excellent source is the public library. Most libraries now have business reference sections where the librarian can give you a very good headstart on gaining information in your chosen field.

The second method is the tried and true one of asking questions of actual or potential customers. In recent years, agencies have been created, both large and small, specializing in this activity. The agencies' representatives conduct personal interviews, send out consumer questionnaires, and conduct panel discussions or seek personal testimonials. In recent years telephone marketing surveys have taken their place alongside existing methods. Because most American households have telephones, it is an extremely cheap and easy way of contacting large numbers of potential and actual customers to obtain facts and opinions. In the field of market assessment there is always temptation to begin to assess opinions. Facts can be had here, and there needs to be careful collation of facts to establish

- Number of potential purchasers.
- Location.
- Characteristics.
- Buying patterns.

Small businesses often believe that they cannot afford expensive market research, and therefore they are at a disadvantage. This is often an illusion. Small businesses, particularly service companies, are more closely in touch with their customers than they believe. A great deal of information can be derived from existing contact; hotels can use their guest registers, shops can review their sales slips and consultants can read over their clients' feedback sheets to establish the basis for a market information system. For the most part, the skill needed here is patience and persistence, to uncover facts.

More difficult, but in the same area of market assessment, is the search for motivations. Motivation research usually consists of in-depth interviews made up of open-ended questions with small groups of potential customers to uncover motivations that can be used either to segment the market or to broaden the base of the marketing effort.

Coverage and Penetration

An important part of market assessment consists of examining market coverage and market penetration. This refers to the company's own position in the marketplace. Decisions have to be made as to whether or not the company will increase its coverage or intensify its penetration of a market. Too often this decision is left to chance, and too often there are insufficient market data on which to base a decision. Much of the grip on consumer markets now being demonstrated by large chain stores and franchises is due to the unwillingness of manufacturers to look at the possibilities of increasing coverage rather than penetration, or reversing the process when faced with attack. Included in this part of marketing information should be: indices of the share in channels of distribution; indications of retail stock levels; identification of competitors' exposure in the marketplace; and, for industrial or investment goods companies, an assessment of the value of different methods of reaching customers.

Product Evaluation

Market research is generally used more to evaluate customers' views of products than to find customers, for here the concern is with product usage. Companies are vitally interested in how the customer sees the product. The same questions arise whether the product is a household detergent or an electronic component, a fast-food restaurant or investment advice.

It is helpful to divide the information required into three parts: strategic, usage, and competitive. *Strategic information* should help to answer the questions as to what future the product now has or should have. *Usage information* concerns the way the customer currently uses the product: its importance and what problems it solves. *Competitive information* should cover not only directly competitive products but also competitive ways of solving the problem.

Strategic Information

Strategic questions are: *Where does the product fit into the customer's consumption system?* This can be either a literal system, such as the way the housewife does the laundry, or a model of how a potential customer deals with the problem of spending or saving money. It can have a literal strength in establishing the size of the container (a bottle, a carton, an appliance) or it can have philosophical importance in establishing the point at which a customer makes a decision to use a certain service (a personal, social perception, view in terms of social and ethical valuation, etc.).

Information is sought to answer strategic questions such as: *What should be the thrust of our product policy in the next five years?* A second, and perhaps more important, strategic question is: *Will the product retain its importance for the current buyers in the next few years?*

Usage Information

Usage information results from questions like: *How does the customer use the product or service?* Very often the inventors or distributors of a product or service find that some users are contrary types who find ways of using it that are not what was originally intended. Human ingenuity, impatience, or perhaps simplemindedness can create a gap between the product designer or manufacturer and the user which should be bridged by information. Too often this bridge is not made, and it is assumed that the service or product is used in a certain way, which in the majority of cases is far from true. Such information is often called customer information, and it can be the most difficult to collect because many people are unable or unwilling to explain exactly how they use a product. If a question in a mailed questionnaire, personal interview, or telephone inquiry is thought to attack a respondent's idea of his or her own self—or if it focuses on a certain human trait such as beauty, virility, honesty, or ethics—then the answer may not be relied on as an honest observation. Most market researchers know this and most market research questionnaires work to avoid this bias.

Two checks that the marketing manager can use on the questionnaire are: First, are there questions which by their implication will tempt respondents to answer truthfully? (A question like "What do you usually do on Sundays?" was answered "Attending church" by an overwhelming number of respondents. When the question was changed to "What does the neighbor next door usually do on Sundays?" a more recognizable picture of life on Sunday mornings of car washing, ball playing, and children yelling was noted!) Second, it is possible to carry out what has been called multi-dimensional research, meaning the possibility of cross-checking the information by some second means, such as observation of actual use.

Competitive Information

Competitive information starts with information that ranks competitors in order of importance, either by their image or their market share. Some assessment should then be made of the competitor's strategy—how they see the market and what their strengths and weaknesses are (in products, prices, development, channels of distribution, and methods of after-sales service). There are, of course, dangers in collecting information about competitors' approaches to customers: Policy can be directed too much towards meeting competition and too little toward meeting customer requirements. A company can be entirely too busy worrying about a competitor's next move to see major changes in the environment. Nevertheless, an awareness of relative market share and competitors' main strengths and weaknesses is an essential basis for evaluating your products.

Consumer Goods Markets

In consumer goods markets it is often worth trying to gain information about the product that puts it somewhere on

Marketing Research and Marketing Information / 29

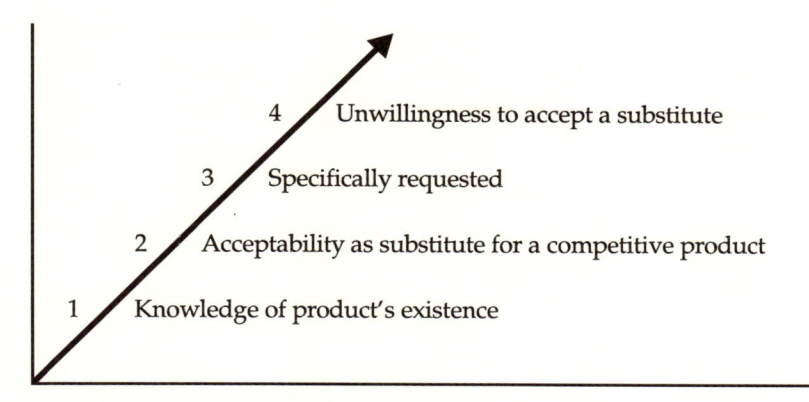

```
4  Unwillingness to accept a substitute
3  Specifically requested
2  Acceptability as substitute for a competitive product
1  Knowledge of product's existence
```

Figure 2.1   Customer Acceptance Scale

the scale shown in Figure 2.1 and constructing questionnaires to elicit where on this scale of acceptance your product is. This can be a valuable starting point for continuing market research; future assessment can demonstrate how far customers have moved along the scale as a result of marketing action (either your own or that of your competitors). Clearly, level one is a basic requirement if you are going to sell anything, and this can be fairly easily established. Level two is more difficult to establish without the more sophisticated techniques of observing buyer behavior or auditing consumers' homes. Nevertheless, it shows significantly more than level one, and is a situation much coveted by companies in both product and service markets that are after the number two spot. (For an airline to be the automatic second choice to the national airline in a large number of foreign countries gives it a very secure foundation on which to build.)

If customers go into stores and request a product by name (by brand, that is), then you have reached level three. The same applies, of course, in industrial markets when your product becomes the standard against which all others are judged—*the* electronic component that fits the socket, *the* part number and type that is chosen for the assembly.

Level four is reached only when you have carved out a niche (maybe the correct term is monopoly), and customers will not accept any other product.

Capital Goods Markets

There are, of course, differences between consumer goods markets and capital goods markets, though many of the same thought processes and techniques can be applied to each. In capital goods markets:

1. There is normally no large homogeneous group of customers; further, each customer may have a number of influencers and decision makers each of whom must be approached in a different way.
2. Although the ultimate purchaser might have an influence on the sale of your product to the capital goods manufacturer, products usually enter the manufacture or assembly of other products before they reach the end user.
3. Products are often selected to strict specifications.
4. Purchasing managers become daily more expert than most consumers—and there are fewer of them.
5. Investigating the capital goods (industrial goods) market is more complicated than it seems. Even though there are usually a standard number of customers, each one will have totally different requirements.

Consumer Goods Markets

There are three different types of consumer goods service businesses:

- *Capital intensive services*, such as airlines, railways, hotels, or cruise ships, where a large capital asset must be profitably employed in the production of the service.
- *Mass market services*, such as banks and insurance companies.
- *Professional services*, such as lawyers, architects, or consultants.

The aim of market research in each case is slightly different.

For the capital asset service provider there is a need to identify (or create) reasons why potential clients should use his service—the objective is to attract profitable clients (or *any* clients) up to and beyond the break-even point.

For mass market services there is a need to ensure that the products match customer needs and are profitable, which involves a clear identification of market segments that can be exploited profitably.

Professional services providers need to create a comprehensive database on their existing clients that will show them, among other things, why their clients chose them, whether they will continue to be a steady source of income, and whether they could become a source of referral for new business.

Marketing Information Systems

The marketing manager needs to have a databank to which he can refer. Such a databank would be fed by a marketing information system. This involves not only collecting information about customers, but also assembling information from within the marketing organization. These data can then be used for planning and control.

To set up a system (or to examine an existing system) there is a need for a few checklists—and perhaps the assistance of an expert systems analyst. The manager should, however, know what questions to ask at the preliminary investigation stage, when establishing the broad outline of the system, and when looking at the output of the information provided.

Preliminary Investigation

The preliminary investigation, which involves documenting existing systems, would look at all information sources and the present procedures for planning and control. An investigation checklist follows.

In so far as *plans* are part of the information system, the following questions might be asked.

1. Are the plans developed in sufficient detail, or are they, because of lack of information, too vague?
2. Do they show who is responsible for results, and is the allocation of responsibilities clear?
3. Do the plans also have activity schedules and timetables, and, perhaps most important, do they have built-in control mechanisms?

Under the heading of *information*, the investigation should look at the following:

1. What information is needed for planning, analysis and reporting, and is that information adequate, particularly for analysis? (Unfortunately, much information, particularly in the industrial field, is sketchy in the extreme, and many managers use out-of-date, irrelevant estimates of the total market instead of finding the correct accurate information.)

2. What internal sources of information are there? Very often internal information is produced in a way that suits the production of the monthly accounts rather than in a way that helps the management of the business. (Control is the subject of Chapter 12.)
Needed is information about

- Sales.
    - –Volume, value, profitability.
    - –Split per product, customer, territory.
    - –Per day, week, month, quarter.
- Salesman's productivity and coverage (calls per order, calls per potential).
- Advertising and promotion costs per product, area, period.
- Deliveries and payments.

3. What external sources of information are regularly tapped? Is regular reference made to magazines and trade journals? Are regular exploratory trips taken to other countries? Are competitors' actions, products, promotion, etc., noted and analyzed? Regular market research should be undertaken covering the following:

- Customers' views and preferences with regard to the product (or better, the problem the product is designed to solve), as well as items such as pricing, packaging, promotion, and after-sales service.
- Buyers' behavior at both distribution level and use level, as shown in choice of brands, types, sizes, or in attitude toward the product or service, or in the image of the company or product.

- Rating the critical aspects of the offer, such as the factors discussed in Chapter 3: product design, price, promotion (both personal and nonpersonal), availability, and delivery as compared to competitors.

Is regular sales research undertaken to examine selling activities in comparison with published data for the industry so as to establish where and how market share is being gained, or lost, or retained?

Under a heading of *coordination*, the investigation should discover whether the documents that the information system presents—plans, reports, statistics—are available to other departments of the business. Much discussion (not to mention argument and backbiting) can be avoided if the crucial pieces of information are passed on to production management, finance and accounting, product development, or R&D.

Looking at the actual *reporting* of performance, the results reported can be matched against plans or objectives (see Chapter 12).

Identifying Problems

In making such an investigation, a number of problems may well become visible. First, sales figures are available, but there is no way in which productivity of the sales force can be assessed (establishing, for example, the calls-per-order ratios, the calls-per-potential usage level, quotations-to-order ratio, share per customer, etc.). Nor is there any way in which profitability can be established—contribution is not easily worked out, profit per product is not established, costs are not known. Second, there may be found to be no monitoring of the effects of a particular mix of products on profitability (usually production profitability—

see Chapter 11) and there is little, if any, cost information on marketing activities. Third, there are no regular procedures for collecting the information required to make reasonable marketing decisions. As a result, it is collected ad hoc, haphazardly, and at great expense. Fourth, the appropriations for advertising and sales promotion are not monitored (see Chapter 12). And fifth, it will probably be found that sales forecasts are confined to the marketing division and are not passed on early enough, if at all, to other departments such as warehousing, distribution, or production.

Using an Information System

A marketing information system is concerned with four main activities:

- Collecting, analyzing, collating, and displaying data.
- Assisting in the process of planning.
- Realizing performance objectives.
- Aiding the monitoring of results.

And there are three major plans for which the information is needed (see Table 2.3).

With the development of computers and, perhaps more, the development of VDUs (visual display units), the emphasis in marketing information systems should be on exceptional reporting. A plea was made some years ago for all reporting from computers to be based on exception principles. Unfortunately, computer printouts are still measured in pounds of weight, and special binders are produced to file those printouts that are no longer in use, despite of the fact that most of the information is not needed as often as it is produced or in such detail, and most of it is held in the computer's memory. Management skill

Table 2.3 Data Provided by the Marketing Information System

Long-range Planning	Annual Market Plan	Sales Plan
1. Consumer data – Age, sex, salary – Consumption statistics – Expenditures 2. Trade data – Channels of distribution – Trends and statistics 3. Economic data – Movements of prices – Raw materials – Legislation, etc. 4. Competitive activity 5. Past sales performance	1. Diagnosis of past marketing data by – products – customers – seasons, etc. 2. Product performance against objectives 3. Product – sales volume – market share – profit 4. Distribution objectives 5. Strategies and objectives per – product group – month – territory, etc. 6. Promotion plans	1. Sales volume per – area – customer 2. Calling rates 3. Coverage ratios 4. Call costs 5. Staff required and costs incurred 6. Objectives of point of sale and other local promotions

can be demonstrated in reducing the quantity of hard copy, while retaining the vital information necessary to make good decisions. Word processors, being memory banks, and modems (for those who have on-line computer access) make it even more important to apply to the above discussion of marketing information the two hard questions: *What do we really* need *to know? How often?*

Checklist of Skills and Action for Chapter 2

1. Do you divide market information into
   - Market assessment?
   - Product evaluation?

2. How does your data bank match up to Tables 2.1 and 2.2?
3. How often do you assess the quality of the decisions to be made *before* asking for market research information?
4. In looking at the product, what effort do you make to evaluate how the customer sees the product fitting into his consumption system?
5. Is your marketing information system based on a complete investigation of sources and present decision-making procedures?
6. Is the information you get from your management information system selected or total? Are there still unexploited possibilities for exception reporting?

3

AT WHAT MARKET SHOULD WE AIM?

Before undertaking market research, or committing very large sums of money to the development of new products, new ideas, or new techniques of distribution, it is important to consider specific markets. Definitions of marketing usually start by suggesting that the market is the deciding factor in the kind of products that should be produced. Businesses need to be realistic about this. They need to recognize that goods are pouring out of factories by the ton. No company can decide to do something different with its products overnight. In service industries, too, real life suggests that no one can quickly change airlines, railways, or banks. Because we already have certain products, some of the markets that we have to choose will be obvious, but their size and their shape need to be considered.

The consideration of what sort of market to choose results from a process called market segmentation. The purpose of market segmentation is to enable a business, by careful selection of the sort of market that is suitable for its products, to both sell and distribute its products more efficiently, and to ensure that the marketing mix that is devised for that market segment is the most effective in terms of both cost and results. Small businesses with limited resources—for example, a bed and breakfast owner, an electrician, an accountant—have an even greater need to select and concentrate those resources on the customers offering the best potential. Thus the more accurate and detailed a market segmentation is, the more likely will the business be successful in its marketing effort and the less likely it is that it will waste its marketing expenditure.

Types of Segmentation

Market segmentation is not a new idea, but it has recently become more prominent in marketing thinking because of the realization that if all products are treated as if they were aimed at mass markets, a great deal of marketing effort will be wasted in trying to promote them. It is thus more important than ever to think through the process of market segmentation much more carefully.

The simplest and easiest form of market segmentation is geographical. Assuming the market to be homogeneous, a division is made between north, south, east, and west; each geographical area is different simply because of its distance from the center, its language, the ease with which salesmen can get around the territory, or the types of distribution. The geographical regions of cities, the density of the population, and so on, can also be used.

In industrial goods selling, a second form of market segmentation is by industry or type of industry. If the same product is used by a number of different industries, then the type of industry that uses it is the basis of segmentation, e.g., lubricating oils are used in heavy machinery, light machinery, original equipment manufacturers, and so on, and this is used as the basis of market segmentation. In services, markets are segmented by types of people who are served, usually by their income level or their age or their social group.

At What Market Should We Aim? / 41

To reiterate, the purpose of market segmentation is to make it easier to comprehend the kinds of markets being discussed. For the most part, the principle is that markets are segmented by their characteristics. Since these characteristics do not change much—markets do not move, growth is slow—segmentation on this basis works well for most purposes. It provides a clear-cut measure for dividing the sales effort, for selecting advertising media, and for distributing the product via the appropriate channels of distribution. There are, however, certain weaknesses in the technique when faced with the need to undertake detailed marketing planning.

There are two further forms of segmentation that should be noted here: demographic segmentation and psychographic segmentation. Demographic segmentation means splitting the market by age, sex, family size, income, occupation, nationality, etc. This is used, primarily in consumer markets as is the second, psychographic segmentation, which is a more sophisticated definition of characteristics and personality traits. "Jet set," "cutting edge," and "nouveau riche" are words reflecting high status; "ordinary folk" suggests basic, economical, "no frills." Provided this is enough information in the title of the segment to decide where potential customers are to be found, how they are to be approached, and what is to be said to them, then there is no need to discuss segmentation any further.

A danger, however, arises in what might be called *post hoc* segmentation; for example, somebody who suggests that if their company has a new filter-tip cigarette, then the market segment they are selling it to consists of people who smoke filter-tip cigarettes. This is true up to a point, but it does not make much difference. What it demonstrates is that market segmentation also needs to show some characteristic about that segment of the market that helps to focus on that particular market segment. Saying that they are potential or actual users of the product being sold is valueless. Thus, in the example, the filter-tip cigarette might be aimed at older women smokers or men in their late forties; that is how segmentation is used.

One of the fastest growing methods of market segmentation—the so-called geodemographic profiling system called ACORN introduced in 1979—operates on the theory that "you are where you live." The basis is the suggestion that those who live in similar types of property, regardless of location, have similar tastes and buying patterns, the information being based on voting rosters, census information, and survey responses.

Much of the work that has been done in recent years on market segmentation has been done in the marketing of consumer products. Under the pressure and influence of media and advertising people, there has been a great deal of thought given to what has been called benefit segmentation. This is a way of segmenting not by characteristics, but in relation to the various benefits that the buyer may be seeking from the product. It could be said that this is just one step from *post hoc* segmentation in that it allows one aspect of the marketing mix to concentrate on one specific aspect of the potential buyer, namely the benefits that are desired. It might, indeed, be a useful distinction for consumer market research purposes; nevertheless, in the early stages it is better to think in terms of motivations. But this strategy may be impossible to implement. Bonoma and Shapiro[1] point out that "buyer needs may only develop in interaction with new technologies which expand buyer opportunities in unexpected directions." (This would apply also to new types of service—consider stores that are open until 11 p.m.) They may, in short, be unaware of their needs until faced with a method of satisfying them (consider the development of new features on cars, TV sets, VCRs, and stereos).

The other approach more generally uses selected market segments on the basis of identifiability and accessibility. This means that segments are constructed using demographic or geographic information or assumptions based on what media are read or seen. The difficulty here is that those who are identified and who are accessible by direct mail or sales activity (or who pass the store) do not necessarily share the same specific needs, or seek the same benefits, though there may be an area of "fortuitous overlap."

This area can be managed by using both approaches together in a matrix form, where the horizontal axis can be used for the identifiability and accessibility characteristics, such as location, age, socioeconomic group, readership of a newspaper—and the vertical axis might be used to identify the obvious benefits sought, or perhaps buyer motivations.

The matrix shown in Figure 3.1 is constructed for the travel market and shows characteristics across the horizontal axis of businessmen, military personnel, sports clubs, women's clubs, artists, etc., being typical characteristics of people who in a certain market are potential air travelers. On the left-hand side of the vertical axis are the reasons for travel or the motivations of such people—business, education, personal leave or vacation, conferences, and so on. A demonstration of the difference between one box and another is shown when considering that a businessman traveling on business by air would perhaps be motivated by the quality of the service and the food and the punctuality of the airline. The same man taking his family on vacation, and paying his own fare out of pocket, might well have other motivations for traveling on a particular airline—such as how the children are accommodated, and certainly what the fares will be during vacation months!

44 / Management Skills in Marketing

Characteristics Motivations	Businessmen	Military	Sports Clubs	Women's Clubs	Artists
Business					
Education					
Personal Leave					
Vacation					
Conferences					

Figure 3.1 Segmentation Matrix

The matrix shown is extremely simple, and the extent to which both characteristics and motivations are segmented depends on the nature of the market to be attacked. It is possible that there will be an extremely limited number of different sorts of characteristics; for example, the market for television cameras (Figure 3.2) can be extremely restricted. In that case, the assessment of motivation becomes extremely important, perhaps crucial, in deciding on the marketing effort to be made.

The characteristics of the TV camera market can be: cameras for television stations, cameras for studios for professional films, cameras used for surveillance, and camcorders used for home video. On the vertical axis of such a matrix would be: quality of definition, reliability, price, availability, etc.

Another important area for using this kind of analysis would be that of a bank's services (see Figure 3.3). For this, the characteristics across the horizontal axis would be the kind of customers—firms or businesses, self-employed professionals, small businessmen, family heads, students,

Characteristics \ Motivations	Cameras for TV Stations	Cameras for Studios for Professional Films	Cameras for Security Surveillance	Camcorders for Home Video	Other Users
Quality of Definition					
Reliability					
Availability					
Price					

Figure 3.2   TV Camera Market Segments

etc. Their motivations would be on the vertical axis: status, the bank where friends do their banking, the bank their father liked, the bank that gives the best interest, the bank with a comprehensive investment package or the bank that is close to home.

Characteristics \ Motivations	Firms/ Businesses	Self-Employed Professionals	Small Businessmen	Family Heads	Students, etc.
Status					
Friend's Bank					
Father Liked It					
Best Interest					
Comprehensive Investment Package					
Close to Home					

Figure 3.3   High Street Bank Market Segments

In many consumer markets the assessment of motivations leads to the sophistication of benefit structure analysis, which seeks to identify the relationship between benefits wanted and received from a product in relation to the product's attributes. The attributes being considered are the features of a particular product that have a bearing on why a customer buys the product. They are not the attributes everyone expects of a particular product. For example, a refrigerator is expected to keep things cold; the specific attributes that particular customers may be looking for in a refrigerator can be: the arrangement of the shelves, the amount of space given to freezing capacity, the accommodation for different types of food, the ease of retrieving food from the various compartments, and so on.

So far it only requires thought on the part of the marketing manager to identify characteristics and motivations in the market segments that he is trying to reach. Once that has been done, then it is necessary to try to assess the potential in each of the matrix boxes. The actual figure that will be found in the box will refer to, for example, potential number of users or potential value of sales represented by that box. At this stage, this is no more than an indicator as to the interest of a potential market. It can, however, provide a useful lead as to the information that might be asked of market research departments. It can pinpoint much more clearly where a market research department needs to look in terms of the characteristics and motivations of the sort of market segment that they should be examining. At the same time, it can indicate where efforts should *not* be made and where the expense of market assessments should *not* be undertaken. As was said earlier, market research should not be undertaken if a decision can be made satisfactorily without it.

Strategies for Segments

Market segments identified by the analysis above can be further investigated by focused market research. The purpose is to identify which strategy might be suitable for each market segment. A later chapter discusses the more detailed analysis required to establish a budget, which is the financial expression of a marketing plan. However, it is possible even at this stage to identify a number of marketing strategies that can be followed.

There is the strategy that treats the market as an aggregate and ignores all differences, assuming that the product can be all things to all people. If you are in a market for soft drinks, or for particular kinds of food, such as Coca-Cola or Heinz baked beans, this is a practical strategy. It makes it much easier to cope with promotional activities, selection of channels of distribution, decisions as to product packaging, quality, etc. Such an *undifferentiated* strategy, though much discussed in marketing literature, is a bit conservative, though it is often used as the basis of global marketing, where the strategy is to pick out worldwide market segments having similar tastes and backgrounds.

A more common marketing plan is the *differentiated* strategy, where a company still operates in all segments of the market, but it sets up a different product and marketing program for each segment, producing perhaps a semi-custom-built product for each market segment. This is most evident in products where there is a considerable amount of export business or perhaps in the automobile industry, where each segment demands a slightly different approach in terms of color, trim, accessories and the like, in what is essentially a standard product.

The airlines have come under much criticism in recent years for having been forced into a situation where they are producing what is essentially the same product, i.e., transportation between two points, and selling it to various different groups of passengers: businessmen, tourists, or families visiting relatives. Each airline tries to make the product look different, but in essence it is the same product. The marketing of the product, however, is totally different for each segment. For businessmen the marketing takes place through travel agents or travel managers; tickets are bought and seats are reserved; there is a possibility of changing the reservation; there is a possibility of canceling the flight without penalty. A tourist, on the other hand, usually buys his ticket as part of a package sold to him via a tour operator and through a travel agent. He often has to buy it well in advance, has to pay a deposit to show his good intentions, and if he changes or cancels his original agreement he pays a penalty. However, he also gets his ticket for the transportation between two points at about half the price the businessman pays for similar transportation.

Another possible strategy is where the company identifies a specific market segment and goes after a large share of it. This is sometimes called a niche strategy and is very often used as a defense against being overwhelmed by a large competitor. An example of this might be a small-town drive-up window, serving a limited item menu like french fries and cokes. Only motorists could access the order window.

Product Portfolio Analysis

These strategies need to be tied in very carefully with the cash flow or cash investment strategies indicated in a product portfolio analysis, demonstrated in the use of the Boston Consulting Group quadrant and well described in an article in the *Journal of Marketing* in April 1977, by Professor George S. Day.[2]

These are the strategies that are predicated upon a quadrant that demonstrates, along its two axes, market share relative to the largest competitor, and market growth compared with the growth of the gross national product (GNP) in a particular country. The quadrant (sometimes called the Boston Box and illustrated in Figure 3.4) is designed to position products or services as one of the following:

- *Cash cows*, whose market share is high compared to the largest competitor, and where market growth is low. The strategy should be to avoid aggressive pricing or product development in the same area. The cash thus generated should be directed to either developing entirely new products or services, or supporting newly launched wildcats.
- *Stars*, showing high market growth and high market share. These require strategies that use the cash they generate for maintaining their own position and profitability; for example, for extra promotion, price reductions, increased production efficiency—in order to pick up potential new users.
- *Wildcats*, showing a high potential market growth and a (so far) low market share. Strategies for these products or services should be aimed at the swiftest possible capture of the increasing numbers of new users—using the cash from *cash cows*. A time limit should be set for checking on whether the strategies are successful.

In static and low-growth markets the attempt to increase market share always comes up against severe competition, because a business is trying to increase sales at the expense of competitors' capacity; but in high-growth markets there is, by definition, a large pool of nonusers waiting to be picked up. *Dogs (or pets)* constitute, unhappily, the majority of products or services in most businesses. Much discussion continues as how best to tackle low market growth and

50 / Management Skills in Marketing

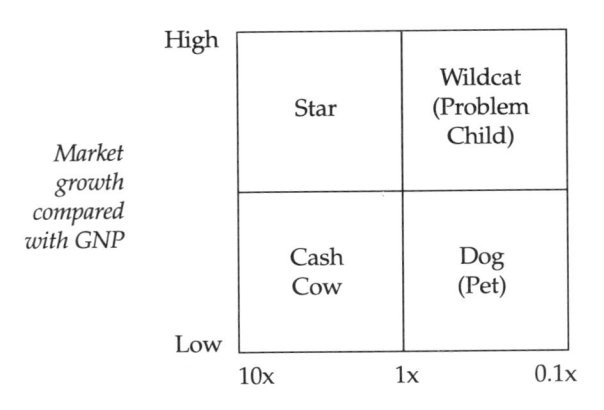

	High		
Market growth compared with GNP		Star	Wildcat (Problem Child)
		Cash Cow	Dog (Pet)
	Low		
		10x 1x 0.1x		

Market share relative to largest competitor

Figure 3.4 Product Portfolio Analysis

low market share. The choice of either abandoning the product, stopping promotional support or selling the whole thing to a competitor seem to be last-resort strategies. A better solution is to try to identify a special niche in the market where a profit can be made by specialization. (A recent example was the exploitation by one company of "the hotel bedroom" as a niche market for 14-inch TV sets.)

The effectiveness of the strategies outlined depends on clear definitions of market segments. If you decide on the horizontal axis showing market share relative to largest competitor, you have to make it very clear first of all what market you are talking about. Are you talking about the market for cars or the market for *executive* cars? Are you talking about the market for soft drinks, or the market for *children's* drinks? Are you talking about the market in Western Europe or the market in the UK? The whole of the product portfolio analysis is based upon an accurate decision as to what market you are referring. Very often, however, this is absolutely clear: If you are talking about oil additives or coffee, then only one market is possible.

Essential first steps are to decide on what market segments you are discussing, not only to define product strategies and cash investments in products, but also to define what sort of marketing strategies to follow. The preliminary thinking about market segmentation is essential; identify market segments and then make the appropriate marketing plans for each segment.

Eliminating Wasted Effort

An additional skill that a marketing manager needs to possess is that of establishing objectives. If an activity is to be successfully pursued, it is helpful if it has a clear and understood objective. (There are two ongoing arguments about objectives. One is that objectives should be set before establishing what is feasible, i.e., that the objective should be set before a sales forecast is made, thus ensuring that the objective is challenging and fits into the overall policy of the company. The other argument states that there is no point in setting an objective without a realistic grounding in what is likely to be feasible; an objective that is set without taking into account what is possible can be extremely demotivating, not only to the marketing manager but to his staff, including the sales force.)

There is little point in setting objectives that cannot be attained, though objectives should offer a challenge. The process of setting objectives should begin with the elimination of those parts of the market where effort is likely to be wasted. Thus, before attempting any forecast of sales in a particular market, the technique known as "elimination algorithm" should be used. (An algorithm [also known as a decision tree] is designed to face the marketing manager with a series of "go/no-go" decisions, so that at the bottom [or top] of the tree is the most logical choice.) A great deal of money is wasted in marketing because marketing managers do not scientifically set about eliminating those parts of the market that will either come to the company naturally or that would be a waste of time to pursue. Thus there is a need for the marketing manager to devise a technique that will enable him to seriously consider which parts of the market are likely to respond to the marketing mix that can be devised and which parts cannot.

The process of elimination will narrow the market into manageable segments and will give a precise indication of the need for more information or more specific effort. Elimination algorithms can be constructed for every kind of market, and can be applied to

1. Market research requirements, as stated earlier.
2. Product development strategy. When considering the development of new or modified products, it is often very valuable to have eliminated whole areas of the market and focused on one specific market segment.
3. Pricing, where pricing is being used as a means of attracting a particular market segment.
4. Promotion, direct sales, or advertising, where it is regarded as very important to avoid waste, or where only a small budget is available.
5. After-sales service, where ensuring the purchasers make the best use of the product is important for repeat sales.

Forecasting Sales

The next stage in the process of marketing planning is to make sales forecasts of the segments that you have chosen, on the basis of other things being equal. Any sales forecast must take into account two kinds of factors: controllable and non-controllable factors in the environment. Figure 3.5

Table 3.1 Elimination Algorithm

Stage One:	Begin the elimination algorithm with the total market. (For most practical purposes the total market can be defined as all those people who are or could be interested in purchasing the product.)
Stage Two:	Divide the total market into groups, by geography, by sex, by income (e.g., towns over 50,000 inhabitants, women over forty, etc.).
Stage Three:	Eliminate the chosen divisions until only one is left. Then divide that in some other way (e.g., those who live in apartments, those who live in houses, etc.).
Stage Four:	Continue the process, eliminating those least likely to be of interest in terms of your product or service by geography (too far from distribution), by motivation (those without gas will not buy gas cookers), by usage, etc.
Stage Five:	Each elimination decision is based *either* on existing information or on hypothesis (the unemployed may not be a good market for vacations). The need to make a decision will demonstrate the requirement for more information—it should provide a clear subject for market research.

demonstrates that these factors can in fact be split into far greater variety than would first appear.

For example, in order to determine the external business environment, look at cultural, social, and economic climate, and political, demographic, and ethical forces and forces that are perhaps totally outside the country in which the market exists. These can be said to be noncontrollable management factors.

Partially controllable management factors would be the development of technology and the competitive climate—partially controllable in the sense that they can be followed if need be, but it is not absolutely necessary. However, you should try to take them into account.

Now in looking at the internal business environment into which this sales forecast is going to be put, look at the controllable company factors: finances, professional

Noncontrollable Management Factors	Partially Controllable Management Factors
Foreign factors Ethical forces Demographic factors Political forces Economic climate Social forces Cultural environment	Technology Competitive climate

Determination of external business environment

Controllable Company Factors
Finances Know-how Plant and equipment Materials Personnel Image and reputation

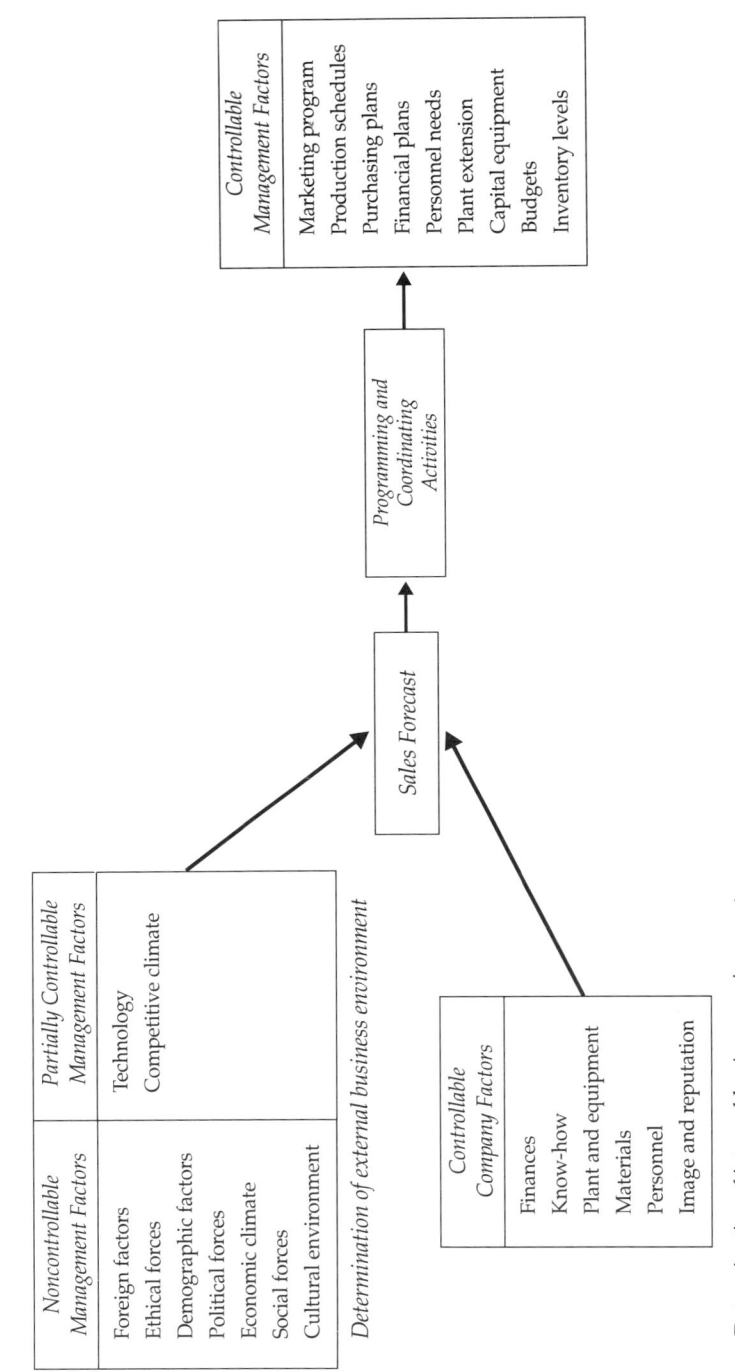

Determination of internal business environment

Controllable Management Factors
Marketing program Production schedules Purchasing plans Financial plans Personnel needs Plant extension Capital equipment Budgets Inventory levels

Sales Forecast → Programming and Coordinating Activities → Controllable Management Factors

Figure 3.5 Factors in Sales Forecasting

know-how, the plant and equipment, the raw materials available, skilled personnel, the image and reputation of the company. Controllable management factors can be then be seen as—moving from top to bottom—the marketing program that results from discussions, production schedules, purchasing plans, financial plans, and probably the requirements for staff and personnel, need or lack of it for plant expansion and fresh capital equipment, together with levels of stocks and the size of budgets, which may or may not be allowed by prevailing cash circumstance.

A major reason for establishing an agreed-on sales forecast is that otherwise all the different operating departments will make their own, based on their own views and assumptions. What the sales forecaster is trying to assess is the weight of influence of each of these factors on the sales he is going to make for the following year.

The skill involved is first to make an educated guess about whether the market segment being looked at and the market segments left uneliminated are worth pursuing. If they seem to be, at first glance, of reasonable dimensions and reasonable profitability, then it is worth going to the trouble of making a sales forecast in more detail. This particularly applies when looking for new markets in which to present an existing product or new markets in which to present new products.

It is said that no forecasting method currently used gives uniformly accurate results with infallible precision. But the fact that forecasts are not accurate does not necessarily mean that they should not be made—but to make them as accurately as possible. The excuse springs too easily to the lips of many failed marketing managers that because the forecast turned out wrong, or the plan proved to be unworkable, forecasting or planning should be given up!

Following are a number of methods that are often used, singly or in combination, in order to try and arrive at as accurate a sales forecast as possible. It is probably wise to check the forecast made by one method against another.

Brick by Brick

One of the most popular methods of arriving at a sales forecast is what has been called the sales force composite, more popularly known as the brick-by-brick method, which is obtained either by asking salesmen's opinions or by asking customers (or by asking salesmen to ask customers) about expected consumption and purchases during the coming year. This technique has a number of advantages, particularly in industrial markets—given a satisfactory questionnaire. If the salesmen have a detailed knowledge of their customers, which is quite reasonable to expect in industrial markets, an adequate result is likely. In consumer markets, however, results are far more doubtful, largely because salesmen tend to have a rather more superficial view of customer requirements; their job is largely to try to sell to customers, not to act as market research analysts. They often fear that if they present a very high forecast to management they will be held to that as a sort of goal. Another factor that can play a role in this form of buildup for a sales forecast is whether or not in the company concerned there is a tradition of asking salesmen for information about the market, about competitive activity, about economic results, about policies, and about changes in customers' methods and products. If not, then salesmen will resent the requirement to make sales forecasts as an intrusion into their activity as customer problem solvers.

There is, however, a way in which some of these problems can be ironed out. This is to recognize that salesmen are either optimistic or pessimistic. They may then be asked to make three estimates: what is likely to be the worst possible outcome, what is likely to be the best possible outcome, and what is, in their view, the most likely outcome. To these three figures a simple formula can be applied, such as the one used to assess operating times in work-study activities, namely: the Worst plus four times the Most Likely plus the Best, divided by six.

$$\frac{W + (4 \times ML) + B}{6}$$

Executive Opinion

The executive committee method, or jury of executive opinion as it is sometimes called, is an attempt to get a broad cross-section of opinion from all kinds of experienced people who give their views as to what sales are likely to be. To do this successfully, it may be necessary to devise a questionnaire with careful scaling on it in order to test attitudes, but it has the advantage of providing a broad spectrum of experience and opinion. However, the disadvantage is that the averaging of "hunches" will not increase the accuracy of the forecast; it may require the use of expensive executive time and will tend to disperse forecasting responsibility.

Arithmetical Methods

The general danger with arithmetical methods is that they make the implicit assumption that what happened last year will also happen next year with more or less the same result, plus or minus a few percentage points. This leads to cynicism on the part of those at the receiving end of a sales forecast, who ask: "Why did we bother to go to all this trouble when all we are doing is simply repeating what we did last year?" For good production planning, however, it may be necessary to plan in detail, down to the weekly or monthly figures, what is expected to happen. An example of this time-series analysis is shown in Table 3.2. The advantage is that with accurate statistics and reasonably simple calculations, a forecast for what will happen month by month during the following year can be derived.

The disadvantages of this technique are that there may be differences in the calendar, there may be differences in price levels, and, although it may demonstrate short-term cycles, it may conceal long-term trends.

Another way that can help to overcome this difficulty is the application of the "least squares" technique to the figures. This will iron out random fluctuations and give a smooth (but realistic) trend line, as shown in Figure 3.6.

The method of arriving at the trend line shown in Figure 3.6 is given in Tables 3.3 and 3.4.

A third arithmetical method often used is serial correlation, which takes the quarterly average of year one, measures the changes that have occurred between year one and year two in items such as cost of living, GNP, tax rates, etc., and applies these changes to year two. An indication of this sort of activity might well be that if year two was expected to show an increase in inflation of 12½ percent, this figure would be applied to the quarterly averages shown in year one.

A fourth possibility in arithmetical methods is exponential smoothing. This formula is designed to give greater weight to the more recent events, and is useful for generating forecasts for standard and high-volume items. This means that sales in the most recent months bear a much greater weight than sales in past months. The formula involves the use of a constant (K), between 1 and 0; in most sales forecasting exercises it has been found that 0.15 is a satisfactory number. Thus in order to produce a forecast of expected sales, the formula is as follows:

K times AS (actual sales during the last period) plus (1 minus K) times ES (expected sales for last period).

Table 3.2 Time-Series Analysis

Column 1	Column 2	Column 3	Column 4	Column 5	Column 6	Column 7
Month	Year 1	Year 2	Moving Annual Total	Moving Average	Seasonal Index %	Resultant Forecast*
January	20	5	470	39	13	6
February	25	30	475	40	75	33
March	30	30	475	40	75	33
April	35	40	480	40	100	45
May	50	45	475	40	112	50
June	70	80	485	40	200	89
July	70	75	490	41	183	83
August	60	65	495	41	158	70
September	40	40	495	41	97	43
October	35	40	500	42	95	42
November	30	35	505	42	83	37
December	20	30	515	43	72	33
					TOTAL	564

*Add 10% to monthly average and multiply by seasonal index to obtain forecast.

Table 3.3 Method of Least Squares Projection

1. Find the arithmetic average of the sales and make this the central point of the line representing the trend.
2. Find the center of the series in point of time.
3. Subtract each period from the central point to find a time deviation.
4. Square the differences and total the squares.
5. Multiply the value of the items by the differences and total the products.
6. Divide the total found in (5) by the total found in (4).
7. The result is the average amount of increase in the trend, year by year, which gives the slope of the line of "least squares" (see Figure 3.6).
8. This figure is added to (or subtracted from) the figure for the middle period (1) in accordance with the number of periods above or below.

Table 3.4 "Least Squares" Calculations

Column 1	Column 2	Column 3	Column 4	Column 5	Column 6
Year	Sales $000	Time Deviation From Mid-year	Deviation of Column 3 Squared	Product Column 2 x Column 3	Trend*
1984	4,050	-3	9	-12,150	4,963
1985	4,700	-2	4	-9,400	5,012
1986	5,900	-1	1	-5,900	5,121
1987	6,900	0	0	0	5,200
1988	5,150	+1	1	+5,150	5,279
1989	4,600	+2	4	+9,200	5,358
1990	5,100	+3	9	+15,300	5,437
$\frac{36,400}{7} = 5,200$			28	2,200	

*Year-to-year increase in sales trend = $\frac{\text{Column 5}}{\text{Column 4}} = \frac{2,200}{28} = 78.57 \text{ (79)}$

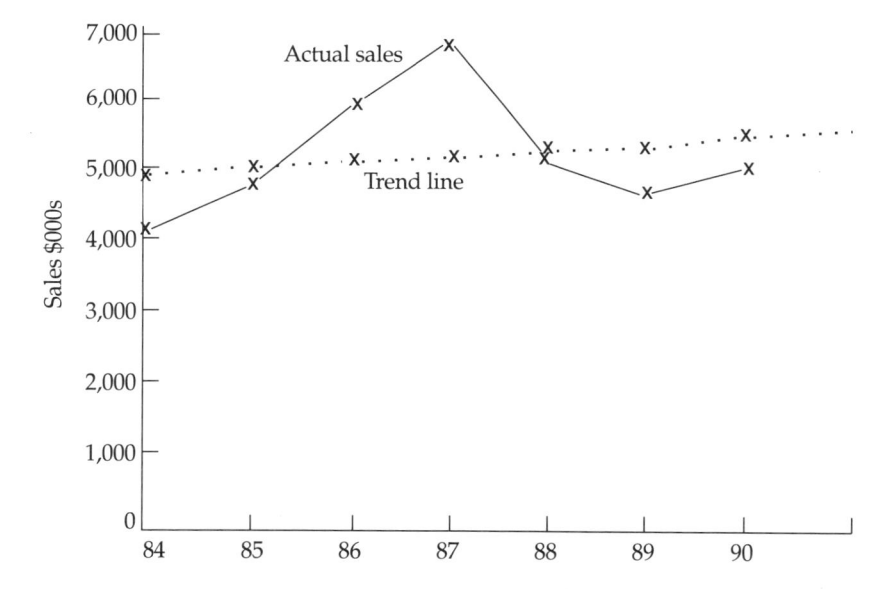

Figure 3.6 "Least Squares" Trend

Example:

$$[K \times AS] + [(1 - K) \times ES]$$
$$(0.15 \times 4{,}250) + (0.85 \times 4{,}000)$$
$$637.5 + 3{,}400 = 4{,}037.5$$
Forecast = 4,037.5

A fifth and very popular arithmetical technique is to use indicators, such as trends or inflation, from sources outside the company, which can serve either as barometers of change or can be mathematically correlated. If, for example, it is discovered that a particular economic indicator has varied in the past directly with the company's sales—an indicator such as the level of employment, the level of sales of a partly related item, or an item that is in some way connected with the sales of your own product—then the mathematical relationship can be used to estimate sales for the future. It is important to choose an indicator that is in fact not a cause-and-effect indicator, but one that over a period of years has been shown to move in a direction that is similar to your own sales.

The last arithmetical method of sales forecasting is probability theories. If a frequency distribution showing past sales is given, and this frequency distribution is sufficiently detailed, unless conditions have changed radically or are expected to change radically, it is possible to estimate the chances of a particular sale occurring during the ensuing period, or of a particular level of sales occurring during one week or one month.

Because the process of sales forecasting is quite often not given the appropriate priority, it may well be a good idea to establish a checklist for the sales forecasting process such as the one in Table 3.5.

Objectives

There is usually considerable argument as to whether objectives should be set before forecasting what is likely to happen or afterward. It is probably worthwhile to consider the problem of the objectives of the marketing side of the business both before, during, and after establishing the sales forecast. What is certain is that it is essential to set quantified objectives for both the revenue and cost sides of the equation. At this stage, therefore, quantified objectives need to be set per market segment for volume, revenue, and (where possible) growth and contribution. These may be split into volume and revenue per product group and the contribution of the product group and volume and revenue per market segment and the contribution per market segment.

Table 3.5 Checklist for Sales Forecasting

1. Collect detailed statistics about sales by product, region, and month for the past one to three years.
2. Make physical analyses of the sales figures in the shape of tables or moving annual total charts, etc. (see Table 3.7).
3. Develop trends from these figures, either in the shape of straight-line projections or using the least squares method (see Tables 3.2 and 3.3).
4. Apply known external factors, such as correlation factors or seasonal factors, to the projected figures for the year to be forecast.
5. Make allowances for changes of company policy or practice so far known, such as new models or designs, advertising expenditure, new outlets, changes in pricing policy or giving heavy discounts, or changes in marketing or sales force arrangements. Assess competitive reaction and try to quantify this in terms of market share expectations.
6. Quantify external factors, such as changes in potential, notable increases in number of customers, expectations of increases in discretionary income, etc.
7. Quantify major external factors, such as rises in raw material costs, reductions in taxes, strikes, etc.
8. Finalize estimate and compare with brick-by-brick forecast.
9. Submit forecast details to "jury of executive opinion."

The detail of what objectives should be set depends a great deal on the marketing organizations, but the objectives given in Table 3.6 give some idea of the kind of objectives that need to be set. In a later chapter costs and how these can be allocated and how cost objectives need to be established are discussed. At this stage it is sufficient to say that they should be set out for consideration with the factors that will affect each market segment. Allocated costs (such as institutional advertising) can perhaps be budgeted at this point.

To help in the process of establishing the dimensions of the objectives that should be set, it is useful to put down some features of objectives that will help in this direction. Table 3.5 showed that objectives should refer to a specific attribute, such as market share, funds available, etc. There should be a unit of measurement either in terms of quantity or in terms of time. The objective itself should be challenging but reachable; furthermore, it should have five fundamental attributes. It should be

1. Measurable and thus tied in with the control and information systems.
2. Achievable, with the resources made available.
3. Credible, so that those who are asked to achieve the objective really believe that it is feasible to do so.
4. Finite, in that there must be a point at which the objective is seen to be either achieved or not reached.
5. Demanding, in that the very highest goal considered is reached.

It is helpful also if objectives can be broken down into part objectives or objectives for units of a larger organization. Naturally the objective units will vary, depending on the industry in which the marketing manager finds himself.

Table 3.6 Typical Checklist of the Types of Objectives to Be Set

1. *Determine contribution and volume objectives*: These should be dealt with separately, i.e., *volume* should be expressed both in units and in revenue, *contribution* should be defined before objectives are set.) Determine these objectives by
   (a) Product or product line.
   (b) Market segment.
   (c) Customer group.
   (d) Customer and order size. (These can be altered or extended as necessary, depending on how easy it is to collect the information required to establish whether the objectives have or have not been met. Marketing information systems mentioned in Chapter 2 should enable this information to be produced easily and regularly.

2. *Determine margin change objective (optional) by revenue created by*
   (a) Price change.
   (b) Channel change.
   (c) Terms or conditions change (discounts, premiums, etc.).

3. *Determine product objectives by*
   (a) New products—numbers, type, launch date, etc.
   (b) Size and range changes expected.
   (c) Packaging — changes, costs, etc.
   (d) Level of service, stockholding, physical distribution, etc.
   (e) Products to be stopped or discontinued.

4. *Determine sales force objectives by*
   (a) Coverage of the outlets.
   (b) New customers expected.
   (c) Customer potential size.
   (d) Minimum order size.
   (e) Recruitment of new staff.
   (f) Training programs expected.

5. *Determine advertising objectives through*
   (a) Communication strategy and objectives of awareness.
   (b) Displays, demonstrations, sales promotion leaflets, etc.
   (c) Participation in exhibitions.
   (d) Production, if any, of coupons, free samples, etc.

6. *Determine channel objectives through objectives in*
   (a) Agents or distributors.
   (b) New channels.
   (c) Improving distributors' standing.
   (d) Training and assistance to distributors.

Table 3.6 Typical Checklist of the Types of Objectives to Be Set (continued)

7. *Determine supporting staff objectives through*
   (a) Market research and information expected to be commissioned during the year.
   (b) Dates and programs for market planning, including special campaigns and the controls of those campaigns.
   (c) Quality of sales office service.
   (d) Delivery goals.

8. *Determine after-sales service objectives by*
   (a) Expected costs per customer.
   (b) Installation of customers' equipment and training of customer staff.
   (c) Costs of service department.

The checklist in Table 3.6, however, should assist in the process of defining what sort of objectives need to be set.

Establishing Priorities—Pareto's Law

One of the major problems with market segmentation and subsequent marketing planning is how to establish priorities and how to assess the allocation of marketing resources. One way, discussed earlier, is to allocate resources in accordance with the potential size of the market segment, (In Chapter 4 the ways in which different factors affect purchasing decisions are considered.) To assist this process and to provide a clear-cut guide to both the setting of priorities and the evaluation of results, the marketing manager can make use of Pareto's Law, which was originally of the relationship between the trivial and the significant and the weight attached to each. (It is now better known as the 80/20 Rule.) Like many rules and laws in a relatively unscientific field like marketing it has to be interpreted fairly liberally—the significant number of customers who produce 80 percent of the results is not always exactly 20 percent; the relationship can sometimes be nearer to 70/30 or 90/10. It can usually be expressed as in the graph given in Figure 3.7, where the line shows the cumulative volume or revenue produced by the number of buyers.

If the market can be assessed sufficiently accurately, then it is fairly straightforward to make priority decisions based on this. For example, this graph can be used to decide which market segments to attack first. Discussed earlier was the analysis of market segments by characteristics and motivations. Some indication of the potential revenue of each segment (perhaps by the market research department) should be able to establish which 20 percent can lead to 80 percent revenue volume. A similar approach can be postulated when dealing with geographical coverage. The location and potential of customers can create a chart giving an indication at least of where it would be prudent to start.

Moving Annual Totals and Z Charts

In these days of computer-generated information (whether by pounds of printout or by VDU) an older and perhaps more personal method of maintaining an overview of current events has been pushed aside. Called a MAT, or moving annual total, it does have its place, however, in the collection of marketing tools that the marketing manager can use.

The MAT began to be used as a way of ironing out seasonal fluctuations, which are a feature of the sales figures in many companies, by giving a moving annual view of the sales results (or invoices, purchases, etc.). Perhaps the major value of this lies in the fact that data presented in this form are rarely available from accounting departments, since they tend to work within the confines of the financial year. An example of MAT is shown in Table 3.7.

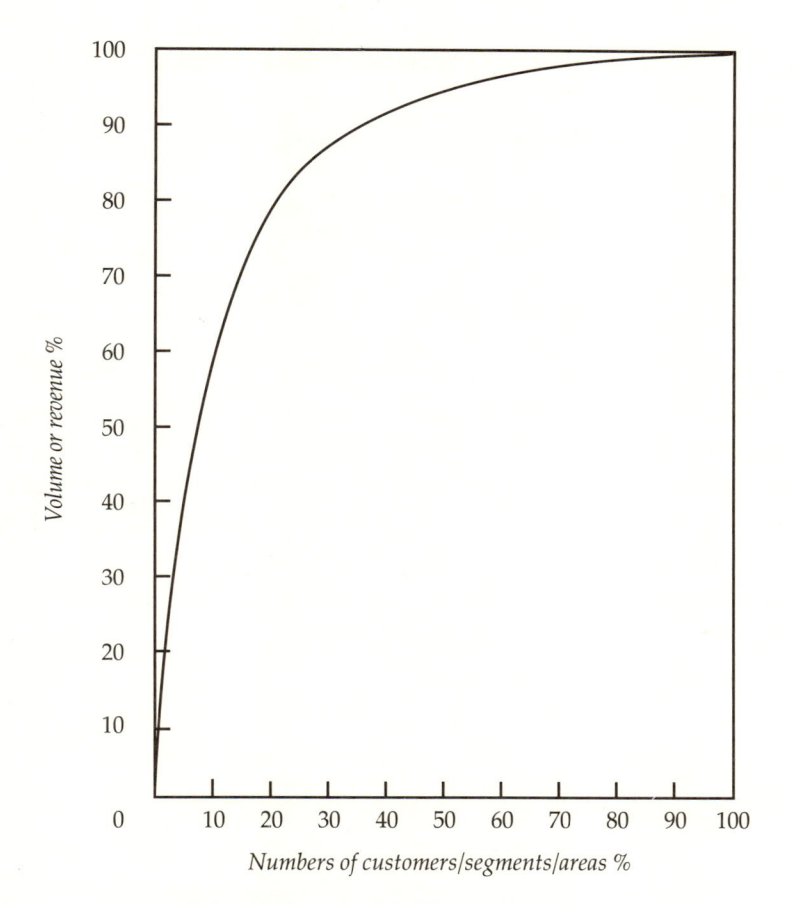

Figure 3.7 Pareto's Law Diagram

Creation of a moving annual total cannot start until year two, and the monthly figures of year one are basic raw material. Starting in the first month of year two (31 January) the monthly sales of January year two are added to the total of year one and the sales for January of year one are subtracted (386 + 12 − 10 = 388) and so on month by month. The MAT is then plotted on the graph and tends to even out seasonal fluctuations, revealing real changes in demand.

In order to create a Z Chart, monthly sales are plotted at the bottom of the graph, and cumulative sales are plotted

Table 3.7 Moving Annual Total

			$000s		
Month	Sales Year 1	Sales Year 2	MAT in Year 2	Sales Year 3	MAT in Year 3
January	10	12	388	13	393
February	15	14	387	16	395
March	30	28	385	30	397
April	32	35	388	31	393
May	34	37	391	38	394
June	38	42	395	40	392
July	40	40	395	42	394
August	31	27	391	29	396
September	40	38	389	40	398
October	38	35	386	39	402
November	36	39	389	41	404
December	42	45	392	43	402
Cumulative Total	386	392		402	

as a rising curve. The eventual effect of the plotting of all the figures shows in the shape of the letter Z (see Figure 3.8). The advantage of this simple control is that most of the vital information can be expressed in comparative form on one easily understood graph. In addition, target or budget lines can be inserted into the graph in advance as reference points throughout the year.

Checklist of Skills and Action for Chapter 3

1. What are the characteristics and motivations of the market segments to which you sell?

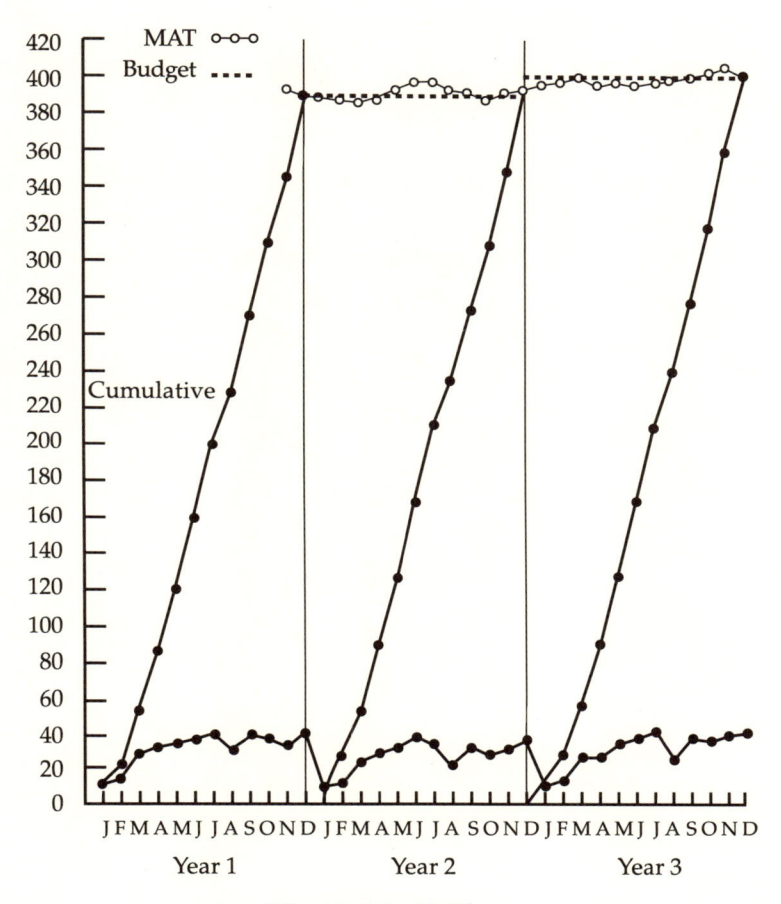

Figure 3.8 Z Chart

2. What is the potential in each of your segments? If you do not know, have you recently commissioned market research to find out?
3. How many *Dog* products are you currently harboring? How many *Stars*?
4. Which markets are the *Stars* part of?
5. Do you regularly examine your effort to eliminate market sections that are pointless to try and exploit?

6. Which methods of sales forecasting do you use regularly?
7. Do you understand the arithmetical techniques? If not, why?
8. Is establishing objectives a regular feature of your planning?
9. Do you establish priorities by the 80/20 Rule?
10. What does your MAT tell you?

4

ASSESSING THE INGREDIENTS OF THE MARKETING MIX

One of the basic functions of a marketing manager is to put together what is called a marketing mix, a special set of ingredients over which he has some control, in such a way that it influences a collection of customers over whom he has no control. Very often, there is no way of knowing what happened in the past and in what way the various factors that are part of the marketing mix might at some time influence the customer. In most companies the ability to assess the effectiveness of advertising, sales promotion, or even the sales force itself is extremely limited. Very crude measures have been used in the past to demonstrate that a company might need either more or less advertising or more or fewer salesmen. No one is suggesting setting up a complete research program in order to discover which of the factors has what effect. What is being said is that there is a need to systematically assess the strength of the factors that can influence the market segments that have been chosen for exploitation.

It is possible to devise a process for this purpose, such as the following:

Step One—List all the possible factors.
Step Two—Assess which factors can influence the specific market segments.

Step Three—Initiate market research (or collect facts) to assess the extent of the influence.
Step Four—Budget input of factors against output of segments (see Chapter 12).
Step Five—Outline activity schedule (action plan).

By taking the steps one by one, a list can be made of all the possible factors that influence a segment.

The Four Ps'

It is probably easier to name the four Ps first under the major headings of the so-called four Ps of marketing: namely Product, Price, Promotion and Place, and then to expand each of the factors to take into account the special circumstances a marketing manager may be faced with in his own company. What we are looking for at this stage is a way of identifying the factors that can be both controlled and can influence the purchasing process. Confusion can arise if there is no clear definition of the sort of market desired. For example, there can be quite a different collection of factors influencing the purchasing manager of a company assembling products from those influencing the designer who decides on components to fit that assembly. Similarly, if selling in a large government-controlled market, it is important to distinguish between the buying factors that might influence, first of all, the issuing authority (such as the Defense Department or the Post Office), the primary contractor, the subcontractors, the consulting engineers, and so on, and then the various decision makers within those groups.

The factors, therefore, should be shown in a matrix, as shown in Figure 4.1. Across the top of the matrix, segments should be noted with a short description or letter. Across the same horizontal axis for each segment should be some

Market Segments

Factors	A					B					C					D				
	1	2	3	4	5	1	2	3	4	5	1	2	3	4	5	1	2	3	4	5
Product																				
Design																				
Technology																				
Price																				
Basic																				
Credit																				
Promotion																				
Advertising																				
Public Relations																				
Selling																				
Brand																				
Place																				
Availability																				
Channels																				
Service																				
Speed																				
Cost																				

Figure 4.1 Factor Weighting

indication of the weighting that should be given each of the factors listed on the vertical axis of the matrix.

The Product

The first factor to be considered is the product itself: its existence, its nature, its attributes, its design and appearance. These can be shown under the headings "technical aspects of the product," "quality aspects of the product," "reliability," "design," "fit into the customer's consumption system" and finally, perhaps, "packaging the product."

If you think about how much the product is responsible for the buyer's purchasing activity, there are very few products which by their existence create a desire in the mind of the buyer to buy. They are found, perhaps, among the basic commodities of food, clothing, and shelter. Nevertheless, it is quite remarkable how many producers believe that the existence of a product will create, somehow, somewhere, a demand. Manufacturers think "If we can make it, someone must buy it." For many of the products that we now take for granted, the demand had to be built up over years. Similarly, an important aspect of the product is its fit with the potential consumer's consumption system. This is true in many domestic appliances and products: The way in which the consumer lives is the determining factor in whether or not the product fits. It is also true in the case of industrial products, which are the raw materials or components for a further product. Nor should it be overlooked in the case of services, where the way in which the consumer behaves can be a very important factor in the acceptability of a particular kind of service. And while considering the factors that influence the buying process, do not overlook the fact that the market segment itself may well have a fairly well-defined consumption system. This specifies not only where the product is used and at what point in time within the buyer's consumption system, but also where it is purchased, through which channel of distribution, and through what sources of information it is sought. For marketing errors are not only made in terms of the design and fitness for purpose of the product, but also in terms of the channels through which it is offered to potential buyers.

Packaging, though relatively unimportant when discussing the matter of gas turbines, has a crucial part to play when discussing food and food packaging. The precise qualities of the packaging material, its ability to keep food fresh, the ease of opening and closing packages, all must have a part to play in the acceptability or attractiveness of the product to the potential purchaser. In terms of services, packaging means the way in which the individual parts of the service are put together. The services of a hotel, for example, are very simple—bed and shelter—but more and more they are packaged into summer vacations, three-day weekends, Christmas or Easter vacations, and so forth. Similarly, banking is seen not just as the ability safely to deposit money somewhere, but as a whole range of personal investment services and advice.

The Price

The second major factor likely to influence buyers is price. The buyer is not only affected by the absolute level of the price, thinking that it is too expensive in relation to what the perceived cost should be, but also its relationship to competitive prices.

There are situations where price alone is the one factor that makes the consumer buy or not buy a particular product or service. In some cases, where competitive pricing is government controlled, the price may well be the only distinction between a number of offers, the specification of the product or service ensuring that the attributes and design of competing products are exactly the same. It may be that the price that has been chosen is a factor of importance to the consumer because it designates the market slot into which this product fits, since there is little other information that can tell the consumer whether or not to buy this product.

Other Price Factors

Factors surrounding the price are also of importance in the drive to purchase; a major consideration could well be the level of discount that can be obtained on the purchase of capital equipment; whether or not the product is stocked by a distributor in the quantity sufficient to enable the producer to provide satisfactory service may well depend on the margin that is offered for the distributor's handling of the product. The development of the very wide distribution of "vacations by air" may well have been because travel agents receive three to four percent higher margin when they are selling a tour package than when they are selling a straightforward ticket. Along with the considerations of distributor margins in relation to price is the ease with which payments can be made by the consumer.

The mail-order business was built up on this basis. Of course, a number of other factors were involved, such as the quality of the merchandise, the ability to deliver, and the spread of agents throughout the country. But what has often been overlooked is the appeal of the mail-order payment facility (the opportunity to buy products and make small payments over time) to a social class whose payment was weekly and what was left at the end of the week was, perhaps, only sufficient to purchase one item for cash. However, if those payments could be spread over a period of twenty-four weeks then four or five items could be bought, and were bought, through mail-order distributors.

In recent years such arrangements have not escaped the notice of sellers of capital goods, who are prepared to lease their capital goods to potential purchasers or to spread the payments for their goods over a number of years. Thus a major factor to be taken into account in assessing the attractiveness of a product or service is payment facilities and credit terms, which are an integral part of the price aspect.

Promotion

The third major factor to be considered is promotion. In many companies, promotion is where the majority of marketing mix thinking is concentrated; in many companies marketing is thought to consist of varying the ingredients in the promotional mix. A number of other factors are also involved; but it is worthwhile to separate out the various parts of the promotional mix to see which of them carries the most weight with potential purchasers.

Within promotion there is first of all, perhaps, advertising, in its earliest and most important role of providing information. An important factor is also the persuasive aspect of advertising and its ability to build images of the product in the mind of the consumer. It has been said that when brands become more and more alike in their physical attributes, the only thing that will distinguish them from one another in the mind of the consumer is their image or positioning in physical or social surroundings. In the same way, an important factor may well be the selection of the media in which the advertiser sets out an offer, together with the message to be conveyed, either through TV, printed copy, or word of mouth. This is an area that should not be taken lightly in consumer goods industries, which are selling, and must sell, in great quantity and at high speed to customers. In this connection the importance of the relationship with advertising agencies is often underestimated. From the initial briefing to the monitoring of degrees of success, the members of the agency must be part of the promotion team. Capital goods selling and services selling is a developing skill that is perhaps underused in the higher reaches of some companies.

Leaflets and Brochures

Another major factor in the mind of a potential purchaser might be the quality of leaflets and brochures. For this reason, money must be spent on producing them on glossy paper with appealing graphics. What is essential is to be sure that the buyer is drawn to this approach and that it will ensure that your product, rather than that of your competitor, is purchased.

In consumer goods selling, sales promotion also has a role to play at point of sale, and in this case it ties in very closely with the kind of packaging that is used. It also ties in with efforts made by salesmen and merchandisers of consumer goods to place the goods so that they will, as it were, sell themselves. Included in sales promotion activities that may persuade purchasers to buy specific products, and may be a determining factor in that purchase decision, are also the activities that are performed in relation to distribution channels. These include the kinds of discounts on quantity, special offers to help goods to be bought in quantity, the availability of stock in a particular supplier's establishment, and so on. In service industries such sales promotion takes the form of offering a service that at the moment is not being requested; for example, a bank clerk asks a client who is making a withdrawal of cash if he has an interest in any other banking services. Such sales promotion might also take the form of suggestions on a customer's bank statement that the bank's services be used as trustee or for financial investment advice.

Personal Selling

Do not overlook the major factor in the purchase process of very many buyers: salesmanship. No one would deny that it is very important, and often the deciding factor in a process of purchasing can be for the individual salesman to come face to face with the purchasing manager or the decision maker to close a deal. It can, however, be overestimated, and too much can be loaded onto the shoulders of the salesman. Similarly, overestimating the importance of the salesman can lead to an underestimate of the importance of other aspects of, for example, the product, the packaging, the promotional material, after-sales service, information leaflets, and so forth. In the list of factors that establish the shape of the marketing mix and the weighting to be attached to each of the items, clearly the personal selling factor carries great weight, but at the same time it needs to be carefully evaluated.

Place

The fourth P in the classical model of the marketing mix stands for place. This includes all the aspects of distribution, not only the channels through which the product is sold—shops, vending machines, agents, distributors, mail order, and so on—but also the availability of the product through those channels, whatever they may be, and, in the case of a physical product or a service, the reliability of delivery promises. How often do purchasers need two or three sources of supply simply because any one source could be unreliable in delivery? In fact, it is sensible for a purchasing agent to do this. Consumers do it all the time; if a favorite shop runs out of a favorite item there is always a shop to go to down the street. Thus examine carefully the role that the distribution channel plays in the decision to purchase a particular product or the product of a competitor—or no product at all (see Figure 2.1 on page 29).

After-Sales Service

Along with other important factors, after-sales service becomes a more important factor in the purchasing decision. Every company, every firm, whether it manufactures a product or provides a service, will establish its own definition of what it means by after-sales service. A general definition might be "all those activities involved in ensuring that the customer is satisfied with his purchase." This would include such items as guarantees, warranties, the right to return defective goods or goods that do not provide satisfaction, as well as all the more conventional aspects of after-sales service such as the repair of faulty parts and maintenance of machinery and devices. In the case of services, it includes the follow-up and evaluation of satisfied consumers to try and ensure that business is maintained in years to come.

Once again the assessment of the effectiveness of this factor in the purchasing process not only helps to determine the size of the budget or the amount of money that should be spent on this factor, but it also allows for assessing the effectiveness of the factor to examine its economy and efficiency. It is the first step necessary in the control of marketing effectiveness to establish the size and weight of the input of each of the items in the marketing mix (see Chapter 12).

Sales/Cost Ratio

For any given product or service, in any given market segment, a different mix of factors will play a different role. It is thus worthwhile to draw a matrix as in Figure 4.1, which will demonstrate which factors could affect identified market segments. Since at an earlier stage we tried to assess the sales per segment, the matrix now begins to show a rough sales/cost ratio. The first attempts at filling in this matrix will be clearly hypothetical. However, a serious attempt can be made to discover not only the extent of the expected sales within each segment, but also the influence of a particular factor on the sales within that segment. Simply ask the market research department or a market research agency to find out. This has the advantage of providing the market research department with a clear and limited view. It enables the market researcher to focus on a specific segment and on a specific factor and to see its effect on that segment. As has been said earlier, there is no point in gaining more information than is absolutely necessary for the improvement of decision making. If the information is already adequate to make a satisfactory decision, there is no point in adding to it. If, however, there is an evident lack of vital pieces of information on which to decide whether a budget should be larger or smaller, or about a particular aspect of the marketing mix, then the market research department should be brought in to help improve the information base (see Chapter 2). Item 8 of the checklist following Chapter 1 can now see the completion of the main aspects of the marketing plan.

Checklist of Action Points for Chapter 4

1. Draw up a chart for your market segments as shown in Figure 4.1.
2. Select the factors that are most important to the buyers/decision makers in each market segment.
3. Do these factors receive most resources—money, management time, effort?

4. Compare last year's budgeted allocation of funds against the factor weightings.
5. Consider reviewing Chapter 12.

II

Skills Involved in Organizing Marketing

5

MARKETING ORGANIZATION

What Does Marketing Organization Involve?

In a book about management skills, there is a need to discuss the whole range of skills that are covered under the general title of organization. Not only does this cover the organization, that is, the whole structure of the company, but it must also have something to say about organizing and putting together, both permanently and ad hoc, groups of individuals to ensure that activities are performed both effectively—which is a measurement of whether the output fulfills the objective, and efficiently—which is a measurement of whether the output shows the optimum use of the input, (or, as has been said: "Efficiency is doing things right, effectiveness is doing the right things").

Because, in its broadest sense, organization is about the framework that enables predetermined objectives to be achieved, this chapter is about the ways in which an organization can be set up and some of the pitfalls that should be avoided. The main pitfall is the idea that because there is a structure, all other problems are automatically solved. The structure is perhaps a guide to lines of authority and an indication of levels within the company, given an (often false) indication of the career ladder. It says little or nothing about responsibilities, relationships, and results (the Three Rs of organizing).

Initially you must know in some detail and fairly exactly what it is you propose to do (having decided on your objectives as shown in Chapters 1 and 3). Then you can start the process of organizing by determining

1. How to go about doing it.
2. What work is involved.
3. What specific jobs have to be performed.
4. What policies will govern their performance.

To complete the step-by-step approach:

5. How specific jobs are to be done, in detail.
6. How people will be found and trained to carry out those jobs.
7. Who will lead and manage these people.

If the organization is to be managed, you will then need to decide how the functions are to be put into logical, cohesive groups, recognizable as departments or divisions, and how, finally, the groupings are to be coordinated and controlled.

Second, although the organization is designed to carry out certain activities so that objectives may be reached, it is fairly obvious that a number of vital factors affect both size and shape (and, with all due respect to the theorists, the structure and operation). Among these are the size of the company and the size of the market. If you are involved in a multinational corporation (perhaps a subsidiary of a subsidiary) and you want to establish your product in a small but growing market, your organization thinking is going to be quite different from someone who has just leased a small factory on an industrial site and is tackling the same market with a similar product.

Third, the nature of the customer is going to have a considerable bearing on your organization. The housewife requires a whole panoply of fast-moving consumer goods marketing—key accounts selling, merchandising, sales promotion, market research, and so on; an oil refinery, on the other hand, requires technical engineering know-how and skill, research and testing departments, contract negotiation, and macroeconomic research.

Fourth, the range and variety of product lines must be considered. Is it possible for them all to be sold by one sales force? Can they be managed by a single product and market manager or should a matrix-type of organization be developed, which is found nowadays in more and more companies?

A typical matrix structure is shown in Figure 5.1. Each product manager is responsible for the contribution of his product line across all the markets that are managed by market managers. These markets can be geographical areas, industries, user groups, or large and small customers, depending on the company concerned; what is important is that the market manager is judged on the contribution of the customers in his market. Clearly this demands cooperation between product and market managers. The three Rs are satisfied as follows: *Responsibility* is for the product line or customer grouping; *Relationships* are essential between the two types of managers, particularly where planning is concerned; *Results* are measured in terms of contribution per product or per market, which should give an agreed total (A + B + C + D = 1 + 2 + 3 + 4) at the bottom right-hand corner of the matrix.

Fifth comes stability or progress—the rate of growth of the company. If the company is growing very fast, the organization will be loose and will change from year to year. If the company shows little sign of growth, or is, in fact, fighting to retain its present size, then the structure will have become fixed and accepted.

The sixth factor is what is inherent in the company—for example, the personality of the founder, the type of

88 / Management Skills in Marketing

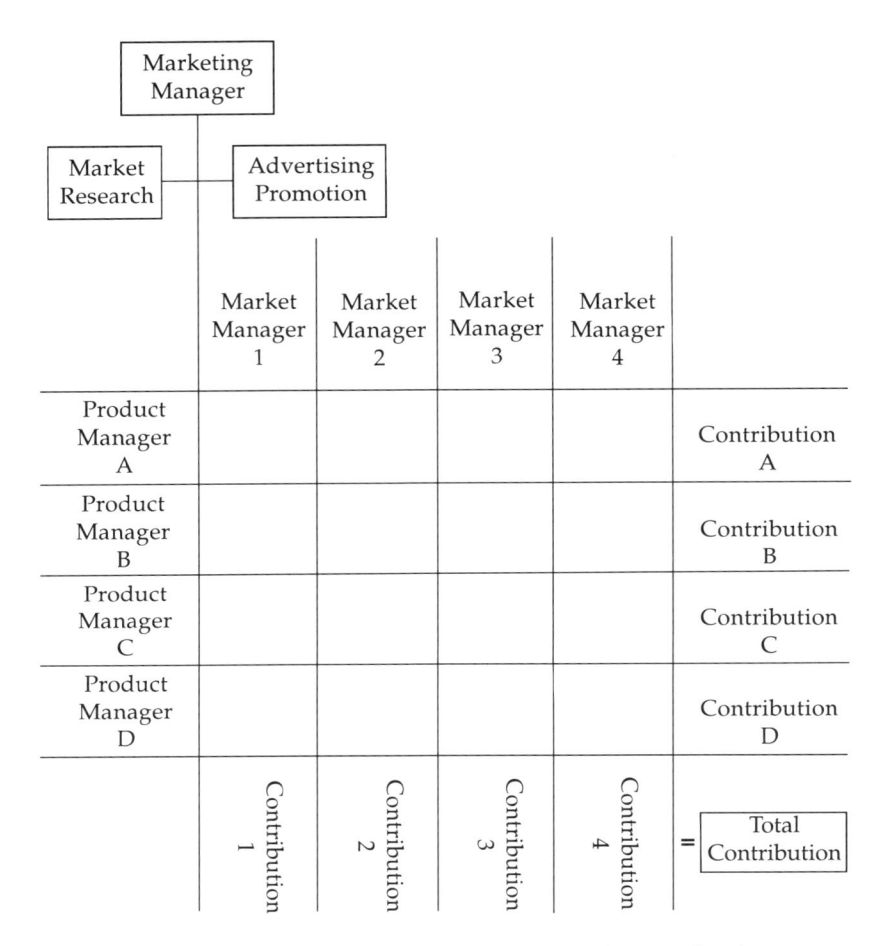

	Market Manager 1	Market Manager 2	Market Manager 3	Market Manager 4	
Product Manager A					Contribution A
Product Manager B					Contribution B
Product Manager C					Contribution C
Product Manager D					Contribution D
	Contribution 1	Contribution 2	Contribution 3	Contribution 4	= Total Contribution

Above the matrix: Marketing Manager, with Market Research and Advertising Promotion reporting.

Figure 5.1 **Typical Matrix Structure in Marketing**

plant necessary to manufacture the product, the way in which financing is organized, the area of the business that requires most management attention because the most money can be made there. Figures 5.2 and 5.3 show these areas of limitation.

Marketing Organization / 89

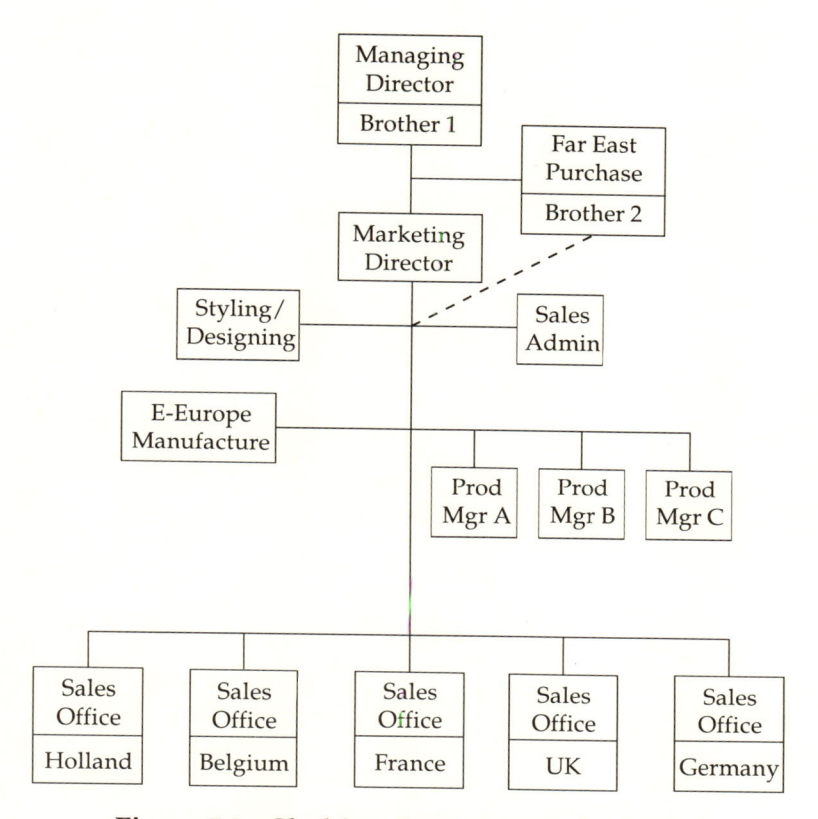

```
                        ┌──────────────┐
                        │  Managing    │
                        │  Director    │
                        │  Brother 1   │──────┬──────────────┐
                        └──────┬───────┘      │ Far East     │
                               │              │ Purchase     │
                               │              │ Brother 2    │
                        ┌──────┴───────┐      └──────────────┘
          ┌─────────────│  Marketing   │
          │             │  Director    │─ ─ ─ ─┐
 ┌────────┴───────┐     └──────┬───────┘   ┌───┴────┐
 │ Styling/       │            │           │ Sales  │
 │ Designing      │            │           │ Admin  │
 └────────────────┘            │           └────────┘
 ┌────────────────┐            │
 │ E-Europe       │────────────┤
 │ Manufacture    │            │
 └────────────────┘    ┌───────┼───────┐
                   ┌───┴──┐ ┌──┴───┐ ┌─┴────┐
                   │ Prod │ │ Prod │ │ Prod │
                   │Mgr A │ │Mgr B │ │Mgr C │
                   └──────┘ └──────┘ └──────┘
```

Sales Office	Sales Office	Sales Office	Sales Office	Sales Office
Holland	Belgium	France	UK	Germany

Figure 5.2 Clothing Company Organization

1. A clothing company run by two brothers, where the emphasis was changing from own manufacture to own design and third-party manufacture plus trading.
2. An electronic components company, where in order to cover the whole market, sales have to be made to both large and small users and also to distributors.

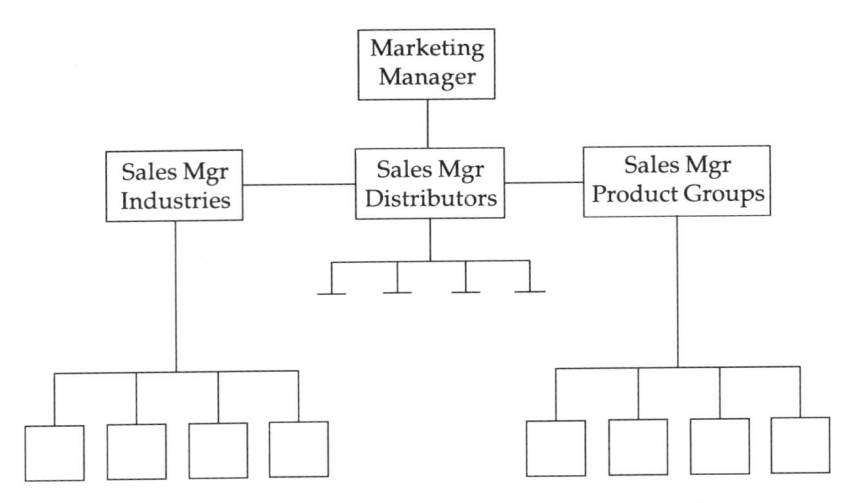

Figure 5.3 Electronics Company Organization

Organization Principles

There are a number of general principles of organization that apply equally to marketing situations.

1. There must be clear lines of authority running from the top to the bottom of the organization.
2. No one in the organization should report to more than one line supervisor, and everyone in the organization should know to whom he reports, and who reports to him.
3. The responsibility and authority of each supervisor should be clearly defined in writing.
4. Responsibility should always be coupled with the corresponding authority.
5. Accountability by higher authority for the acts of its subordinates is absolute.
6. Authority should be delegated as far down the line as possible.
7. Levels of authority should be kept to a minimum.

8. The work of each person in the organization should be confined as far as possible to the performance of a single leading function.
9. Whenever possible, line functions should be separated from staff or specialist functions, and adequate emphasis should be placed on important staff activities.
10. Limit the number of positions that can be coordinated by a single executive.
11. The organization should be flexible, so that it can adjust to changing conditions.
12. The organization should be kept as simple as possible.

To summarize, there should always be a single chief marketing executive responsible to the managing director (or CEO) of the organization for the effective conduct of all the operations entrusted to the marketing function.

Types of Organization

Although there are a number of variants, and each organization is different from another to some degree, there are two main ways that functions or tasks can be split up: by geography or by specialization. When an activity becomes too large for one person it can be divided either into two similar functions—one taking the Western division and the other taking the Eastern division, or one doing the selling, the other doing the production.

Most large companies have both forms of division, and the manager has to consider not simply the functions, but how they relate to each other and how the systems work. For example, dividing the country into sales areas is a fairly common way of organizing the sales activity, each area having a salesman in charge. If at the same time the product management activity is divided into specialist product groups, each with a manager, then the relationship between the company and the customer becomes more complicated, because a product manager is usually given responsibility for the profitability of his product, while the salesman is given responsibility for the results of his customer (see Figure 5.1).

A totally functional organization, with each specialization being separately handled, usually exists only in small companies; there is in this case a sales manager, order-handling manager, market research manager, advertising manager, distribution manager, and service manager—all responsible to the chief marketing executive.

However, as soon as different products or different markets become important, a different set of relationships is necessary. Effectively, the matrix organization as shown earlier in this chapter comes into operation, though in its early stages it is heavily disguised.

If the weight of the activity takes place away from head office, then marketing gets dispersed and becomes the local operating creed. Central staff departments begin to proliferate, whose strength depends on their ability to influence those operating at the customer level. There are companies that, in general, are as shown in Figure 5.4 (general because this is an oversimplification of the relationships). Basically, the regional managers have total authority for marketing decisions within their region. Their power is limited only by the availability of the right product from the factories. The product managers, serving on the marketing staff, are supposed to act as liaison between the two. Note, however, the organizational and structural groups that exist with this structure as compared with the matrix type structure shown in Figure 5.1.

Another form of organization that affects many multinational corporations seems to put the product manager

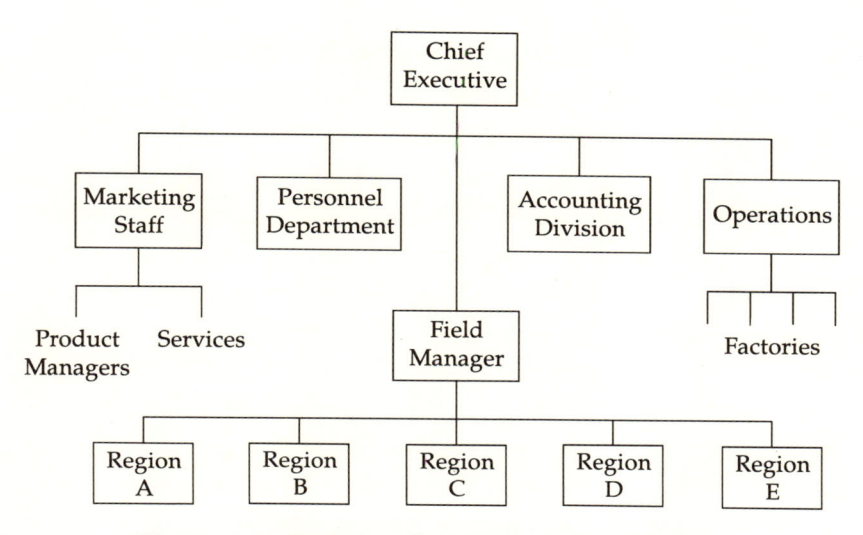

Figure 5.4 Weight of Activity in the Regions

in an even more difficult position. Effectively, the structure looks like that shown in Figure 5.5. The task of the local product manager is to interpret the centrally produced products for the local marketplace.

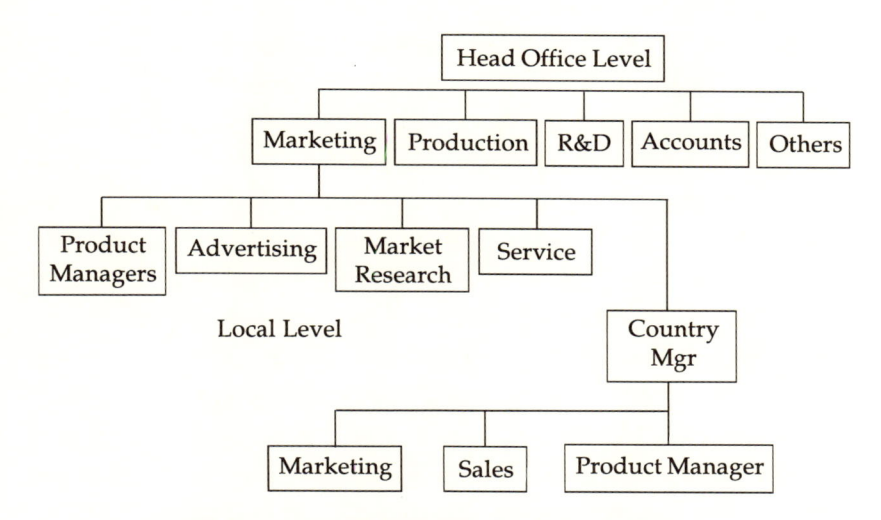

Figure 5.5 Product Manager's Position

Relationships and Systems

Since organizations are designed to accomplish activities so that objectives will be reached, it is important to consider both relationships and systems. The easiest relationship to describe and understand is the direct executive one, which is the direct control of one individual by another to create a direct channel of command. Salesman-sales supervisor-sales manager is such a direct-line relationship. It is a line of authority and accountability. The more difficult relationships grow from the need of the business to have functional specialists who have responsibility for certain results, without being in direct control of some of the people who create those results. They can be managers who give advice, who assist, or whose functions overlap, for example, market research managers, sales promotion specialists, or credit controllers. If they need the services, time, knowledge, or cooperation of the sales force, they have to achieve this *either* by invoking the official line authority of the boss, or by informal contacts, which carry little authority.

One of the best ways of solving this problem of relationships is to look at the different systems that operate and try to manage them as systems rather than trying to boss the people. There could be a new product development system that involved a whole collection of different people in different departments; there could be a marketing planning system that started with the collection of information and forecasts from salesmen and finished with the submission of the marketing plan to top management. Each system could be drawn out and would, if managed properly, allow the relationships in the organization to fit into the agreed system (See Table 5.1.) (Figure 5.6 shows a dynamic representation of a forecasting system and a collection buildup system, both of which were identified as the important operations of the garment manufacturer in Figure 5.2).

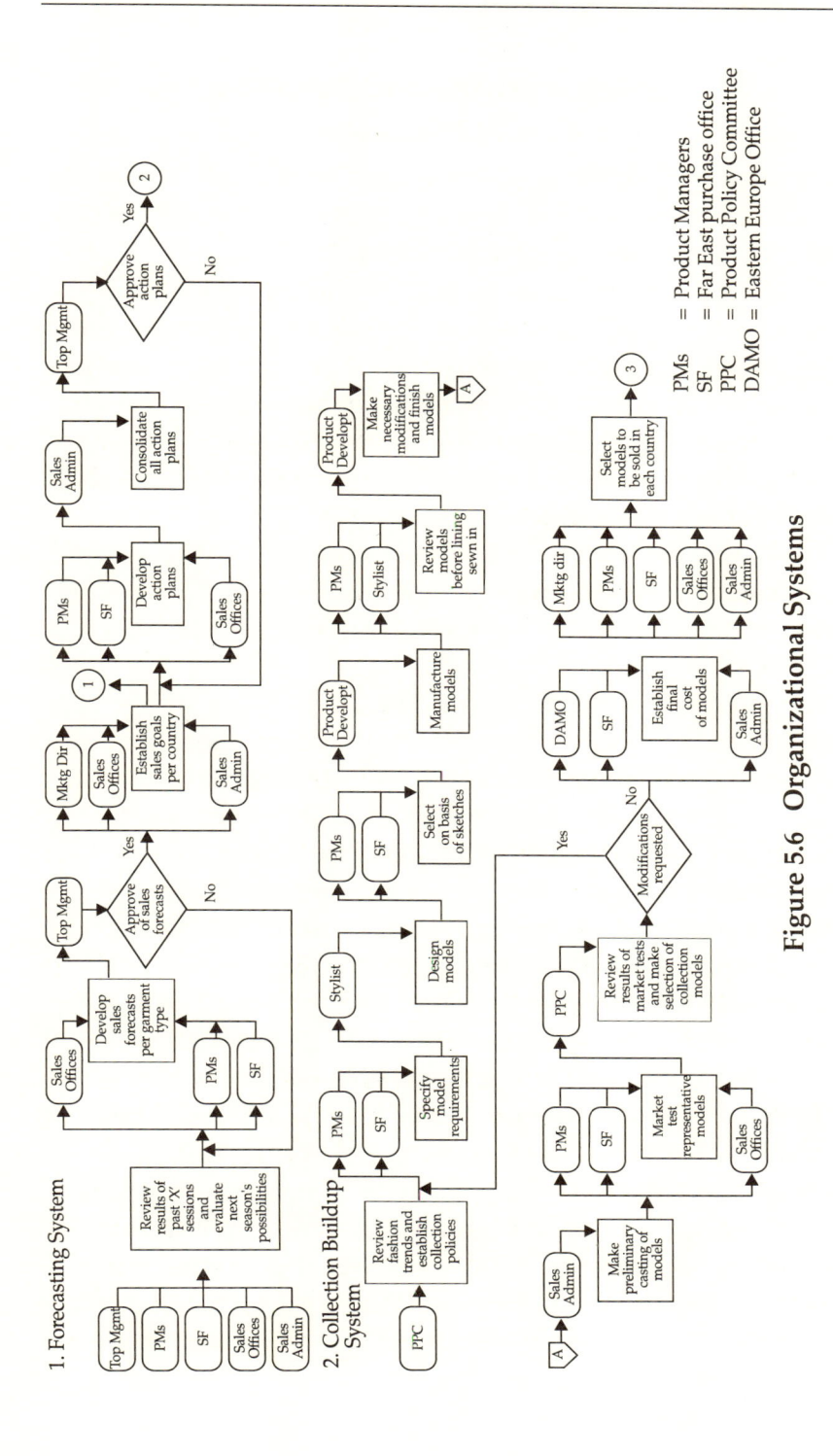

Marketing Organization / 95

Figure 5.6 Organizational Systems

PMs = Product Managers
SF = Far East purchase office
PPC = Product Policy Committee
DAMO = Eastern Europe Office

Marketing Activities and the Place of Sales Operations

Marketing operations have two different kinds of activity within them: business building activities and service activities, i.e., the routine operation of the business.

The primary business building activities within the marketing organization are sales operation and advertising. Without a sale, all activities of the business are just costs. Nevertheless, the relationships between sales operations and the planning and support functions need careful study. The profitable marketing organization tends to be a well-balanced operation.

How, under modern circumstances, are the various marketing activities related organizationally to sales operation? The activities most frequently listed are shown in Table 5.1.

In earlier marketing thinking, sales were straightforward order getting. When getting the order became more elaborate, additional functions were grafted onto the sales manager's function until this became almost impossible to carry out. A key factor in accomplishing the change was the discovery that selling out from the retail outlet is just as important as selling in. A more modern separation of functions then established itself by degrees. It may be described as customer-oriented organization. This is reflected in the changes from Figure 5.7 to Figure 5.8.

The success of the customer-oriented organization depends on effective integration at the level of the salesmen in the field. The modern sales manager's prime function is to ensure that creative selling contacts of proven constructive form are taking place regularly in all profitable outlets. These outlets may be grocery stores or oil refineries, the contacts may be made by managing director to chairman, salesman to purchasing officer, or service engineer to main-

Table 5.1 Marketing Activities

Input or Support Activities	Executive Activity of Marketing	Output or Control Activities
Long-range marketing planning		
Marketing research		
Brand management		
Product planning		
Advertising		Profitability analysis
Merchandising		Distribution cost analysis
Sales promotion and PR		
Packaging	Sales operations	Sales performance control
Pricing		
Warehousing and transport		Administration, internal and external
Licensing and patents		Records
Channels of distribution		
Sales statistics and budgets		
Servicing		

tenance foreman, but all these contacts should come within the purview of and be coordinated by the selling company's sales manager. At the same time, whoever makes the selling contact should be confident that the selling company's advertising, distribution, servicing, pricing, etc., have all been carefully planned. This is the task of the selling company's marketing director or manager.

98 / Management Skills in Marketing

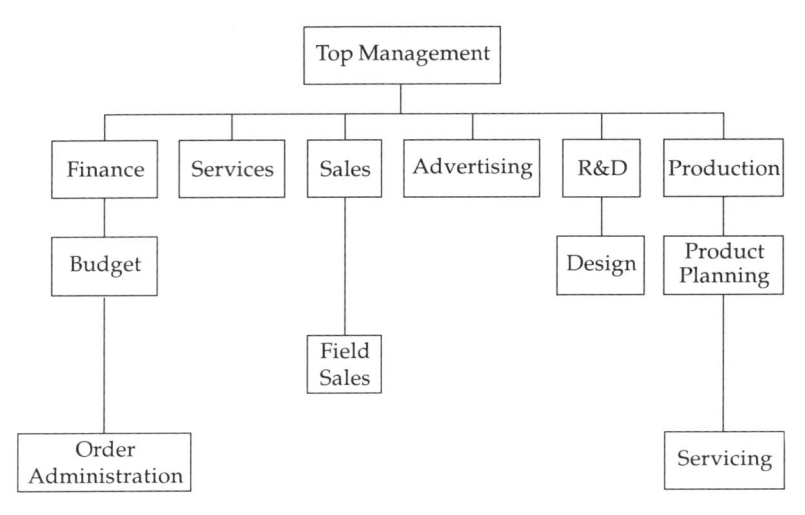

Figure 5.7   Traditional Pattern

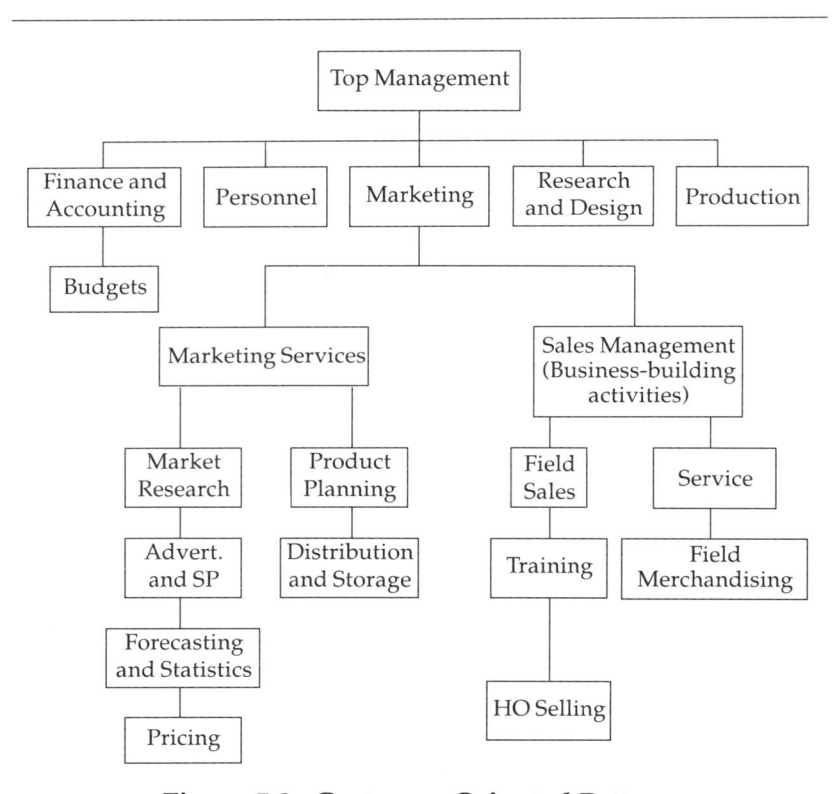

Figure 5.8   Customer-Oriented Pattern

Checklist of Action Points for Chapter 5

1. Does your marketing organization work?
2. Has it been looked at in the last five years?
3. Has it been changed more than once in the last five years?
4. Is there an overload on executives?
5. Are communications good? (See Chapter 9.)
6. Is the management information system operating
   - At all?
   - Rarely?
   - Well?
   - Overwhelmingly well?
7. Are decisions carefully thought through?
8. Are there forecasts and plans?
9. Are there clear objectives?
10. Is there delegation?

6

IMPROVING MANAGEMENT PERFORMANCE

One of the skills that all managers should possess is that of motivating their employees and one of the best ways to achieve this is by using the techniques of management by objectives. In spite of the disillusionment of those who expected a new gospel and found only organized and systematic common sense, there remains an essential and underlying foundation that is constantly being added to and developed by practical experience in many companies and in different management functions. Very few major companies operate today without a framework of agreed-on objectives and planned appraisal systems.

Starting Points

The company's objectives and the needs of the individual must be integrated if the organization is to function efficiently. The problem is how best to do it. In the past, the problem was only dimly perceived, since the tasks of entrepreneurs and workers were quite clearly defined. But with the rise of what Galbraith calls the "industrial technostructure," the development of large organizations with large numbers of middle managers, and with the rising educational standards of the work force, a credibility gap has become painfully obvious. It was Mary Parker Follet who rejected compromise in favor of integration in the clash of conflicting views, and here the process of integration is carried through a company systematically from top to bottom.

Before there can be any planned appraisal systems there must be objectives. The setting of company objectives is a hard intellectual exercise. It means cutting through phrases like "to make a profit" and getting down to hard facts. There are many illustrations of the fact that firms share as an objective a very strong drive toward continuity and the provision of employment, with a secondary aim of providing profits for their shareholders. Indeed, in thinking about objectives, it is often helpful to draw up a dependence diagram. If a business is concerned about surviving at least for the next ten years, then it requires finance. Finance depends either on borrowing (and there are certain basic requirements for that), on making profits, or on both. Profits in their own right depend on making efficient use of assets and, in high labor cost industries, on growth. Thus, we can build up a hierarchy of objectives for the company, and if necessary quantify them.

Role of Marketing

As was discussed earlier, the role of marketing in the setting company's objectives is crucial. After all, it is marketing that produces results, all the other activities of the company produce only risks or costs. Marketing is concerned with balancing what the customer wants with what is profitable for the company. This is the marketing concept. Marketing contributes to the company objectives in the areas of

- Market standing (what is and should be the company's share in existing markets).

- Product development (what new products will be needed within the company's existing framework, to maintain or strengthen its present position).
- Entry into new markets (where and in what way new markets can be entered with existing products or possible new products).
- Return on investment (what return on investment can be expected and anticipated over the next five years).
- Growth rate (how fast does the company need to grow, for its own profitability and to match its competitors).

If these objectives can be set and (once again) quantified, then the unit objectives follow without difficulty. The major objectives are translated either for a product group, such as the group manufacturing and selling industrial paper stock in a paper-making company; or a functional group, such as the marketing group in a company not having a product grouping; or a geographical group, such as the subsidiary organization in a particular country. A large international group that has all three units—product groupings, functional services, and a geographical responsibility—must ensure that the objectives for each unit are integrated.

The objectives are then passed down to individual managers—sales managers and salesmen, for example. In the sales field this becomes even more important than in other parts of the company, as the salesman's task has management functions in it.

An objective to increase market share by a certain percentage is translated into the following three aspects:

- Policy—the way in which the market share is to be increased, such as expanding distribution outlets, increasing order size, or changing packaging.

- Execution—detailed planning of programs to be carried out, schedules of sales activity, or advertising media.
- Standards of performance—the measure of how well plans are carried out, policies are followed, and objectives are reached.

It is at this point that the mechanistic approach to management stops, in the belief that everything has been done to make things happen, even though for many years now the problem of motivating people to work well has been exhaustively discussed. The major complication of motivation has always been that individuals are motivated in different ways. In spite of the discoveries of psychologists that there are general motivators (satisfiers and dissatisfiers), the strengths of these in each individual vary. General motivators (such as money) have different effects on people.

Nevertheless, there remains a need to find some way in which to induce individual managers and their employees to work toward the objectives of the company, and to seek improvement in both organizational work methods and organizational goals.

Management Development

Many management development schemes and performance appraisal systems have failed as a result of underlying faults. These systems are designed with care and carried out conscientiously but they fail either to motivate people or promote the right people for more responsible positions. A number of reasons can be seen for these failures, including

1. Employee objectives are different from company objectives. This can result from top management not

having done its homework in setting the company's objectives clearly and passing them down the line, or it can simply be that no one has ever discussed with the manager or employee what his objectives should be. Many managers are still judged on how busy they are, not on what results they achieve; many salesmen are judged on numbers of calls or sales volume rather than product mix or profitability.

2. Failure to give sufficient weight to performance and the production of results in selection processes. Ratings are too often made on personality traits, if the person gets along well with other people or other intangibles, and too rarely on the straightforward achievement of results.

3. The belief that by setting up an appropriate management development or sales training program the right people with the right answers will be there—a stream of qualified people with management potential who have only to be slotted into the right areas.

4. The idea that perhaps the problem of management can be solved by recruiting young graduates, or the expansion of the sales force can be accomplished by hiring trained staff from competitors. What has been called the Crown Prince complex brings with it as many problems as it solves. The graduates become disenchanted because they are promised too much in the early stages and the company has not considered how it wants to integrate them with the rest of management. The experienced salesmen bring with them not only the expertise but also the faults, the differences in policy, the unacceptable work methods of competitors, all of which take a long time to unlearn.

5. Promotion as a ladder, not an escalator. The exaggerated emphasis on promotion as the target for

ambition causes many managers (and salesmen) to concentrate on the next step up, rather than on improving performance in their present job.
6. Managers abdicate their task of managing personnel to a personnel department. This leads to the situation where industrial relations officers are standing between the manager and his employees, with a major part of the manager's responsibility disappearing.
7. Finally, the belief that managers can be developed by some kind of applied process, which is the greatest mistake of all. Good managers grow in an organization, if they are allowed room to breathe.

The Manager's Needs

With the faults of management development programs in mind, this next approach to managing looks at the real needs of the manager or of any employee, as this applies equally to a salesman who is a "mini-manager."

The first need of any employee is to know what he is expected to do; but there is a deeper need than this, a need for involvement in what is expected of him, a share in the process of decision, a mastery of his fate. It is found that if the outlines of the task are arrived at after discussion and agreement the employee probably works better.

A second need of managers in responsible positions is to be allowed to exercise their skills, to carry out their responsibilities, to be allowed the opportunity to perform.

A third need is the need to know how one is doing in the opinion of the boss—and, indeed, by an objective standard.

A fourth requirement of managers is to have and provide help and guidance. No one will ask for assistance or support if he has been told to get on with a job; but if by a process of discussion and agreement certain performance standards have been arrived at, then part of the discussion will center on whether the manager or employee can perform his part of the bargain, or if he needs help with it.

Finally, the manager needs to have and to provide recognition. Recognition means more than a pat on the back: It means the whole spectrum of pay and promotion according to his contribution.

Job Analysis

To meet the requirements of the individual, the process sets out to try to ensure that the aims of the individual fit with the objectives of the organization in two ways: a structured discussion between an employee and his boss, and a simple form that records the results of that discussion. In fact, a form is not really necessary as long as the structure of the discussion is simple.

To describe the structure of the discussion, it is perhaps easiest to take the manager's basic needs and set them in a management guide (See Figures 6.1 and 6.2).

The first part of the form covers what the job is all about: its purpose, where it fits in the organization structure, and current short-term priority tasks. Even here the opportunities for clarification are considerable if the employee and his

---

Job Title
- *Main Purpose of the Job*
- *Position in the Organization*
    - Person directly responsible to
    - Employees directly supervised
    - Other colleagues with whom frequent contact is made
- *Current Areas of Job Concentration*

Figure 6.1 Management Guide (Front Page)

Key Task	Standards of Performance	Controls	Suggestions for Improvement

Figure 6.2 Management Guide (Main Part)

boss each write down their ideas on these matters. Brought together, the two documents often show a remarkable (and, all too common) divergence of view on the purpose, priorities, and objectives of a job. But this hardly differs from the opening sections of a conventional job description. It is when the second part of the form is complete that its real value becomes apparent.

Key Tasks

The second section of the form allows the employee and his boss to identify the five or six vital result areas of the job (key tasks), answering the question: What are the really important things the employee is expected to achieve in pursuit of the organization's objectives? Because the concentration is on the results to be achieved, how the result is achieved nor how well it is done is described here. Naturally, key tasks will differ from job to job, but some typical ones for a salesman might be to

1. Achieve his personal sales quota.
2. Sell the fullest possible range and quantity to individual customers.
3. Plan site visits and callbacks so as to achieve the maximum practicable selling cost.

4. Make new customers.

5. Make a sales approach of the required quality.

In each of these a clear result is implicit in the description. Once again the identification of vital result areas is not easy, but given an emphasis on *vital* and *result* the task becomes more meaningful.

Salesman's Example

Key Task Two—To sell the fullest possible range and quantity to individual customers.

Agreed Standard—At least ten cases each of Pepsi, Coca Cola, and Shasta brands to be sold to Lucky, Von's, and Big Bear before 30 June.

Key Task Four—To make new contacts.

Agreed Standard—Ten entirely new customers place orders for at least fifty cases in the three months ending 30 September.

Performance Standards

An essential part of any task is to set down the conditions that would apply when the task was being done well—described as standards of performance. Although a task can be described in detail, if the level of performance for that task is not agreed on then the effort of description is wasted. If running a mile is a vital result area for an athlete, then it is of great importance to know if the mile has to be run in under four minutes, exactly 4½ minutes, or no more than five minutes. Such a standard will vary from athlete to athlete and will depend on the conditions of the race.

Standards should be agreed on with employees in quantitative terms: in terms of time, the time that a job must be completed or a level reached; and in terms of quantity, how much must be accomplished or how many tasks must be completed. In many jobs there is also a qualitative element:

how well does the task have to be performed? For example, personnel selection must be good enough to ensure that labor turnover is less than a certain percentage per year.

In establishing a standard a number of the more vague expressions common in job descriptions must be avoided. Such words as "adequate," "approximate," "appropriate," "reasonable," and "desirable," are always capable of different meanings, depending on the viewpoint of different people. Likewise, we have all met that all-embracing phrase "as soon as possible," which can mean tomorrow, next week, next year, when your turn comes, when there is nothing more important to do, or when the store manager gets around to it!

Delegation

"Give me an opportunity to perform." In many companies this is one of the most difficult tasks to accomplish. Managers are reluctant to delegate, and even when they are forced to do so by pressure of workload, they do not delegate properly.

A brief anecdote illustrates this. A manager delegates to his secretary the task of making coffee for him. If he tells his secretary precisely the blend of coffee he requires, the shop to buy it from, how long it should be percolated, and the precise times during the day when he needs it, delegation is non-existent. If, however, he tells his secretary to make a pot of coffee at specific times during the day, then he has fully delegated the task.

Nevertheless, the process of delegation is one of trusting the employee to produce the agreed on result, and giving the employee the chance to do the job on his own.

Controls

"Tell me how I'm doing." Following from delegation is the need of the individual to know whether or not his performance is up to standard. So the third column of the form is headed Controls. Against each performance standard is listed the control by which that performance can be measured. There are two kinds of control mechanisms: documentary and visual. Documentary controls, include sales control statements: volume and value, sales costs, reports on market or competitors, budget statements, and reports on sales calls. Visual controls include inspection, observation, spot checks, and perhaps comments from others—and, in the case of a salesman, perhaps customer reactions.

Controls often exist, but they are often designed to fit with accountancy requirements, not with the need of the employee and his boss to know how well the agreed on standards are being met. Both manager and employee are trying to judge when things are not right; if no information exists, then judgment is bound to be subjective and colored—both the boss's judgment of the performance of his employees and the employee's own opinion.

Improvement

It is in the fourth column of the form that the need "Give me help and guidance where and when I need it" is covered. Having looked at the job in some detail, the intention is to find areas where performance can be improved. Against each key task, in the experience of most people who have gone through this procedure, there will come a number of suggestions for improvement; for example, there will be areas where help and guidance is needed, either directly from the boss or through training; areas where there are organizational obstacles to performance or wrong standards; and areas where, through the inadequacy of others, standards cannot be reached—for example, the lack of prompt deliveries that prevent the salesman from reaching his target.

Action Plans

The finalization of the management guide leads inevitably to action plans for both employee and boss. Action plans should list those things that need to be done to improve the employee's performance—for a salesman, perhaps focusing on improving product knowledge, or more careful planning time to allow for new account prospecting; for the boss, covering what he needs to do to help and guide his employee to smooth the employee's path to the objective. Action plans must always include a time limit. The action specified must be carried out by a particular date, and on that date some control mechanism should signal the completion and the success or the failure of the action.

Review

In all systems—and although this is not a system in the literal sense, it still has systematic features—there needs to be a feedback mechanism to complete the loop. This is the review. Even though the employee and his boss are in regular, perhaps daily contact, there is still room for a regular meeting every so often, perhaps every three months or every six months, to discuss how the employee's task is being performed. At the very least, if each man has gone through the difficult soul searching required to build up a good job results guide, then a review of performance can justify that effort. This is an essential stage in improving performance. It is a natural development of the style of managing that involves discussion and agreement between boss and employee over the objectives, over the vital result areas and standards of performance, and over opportunities for improvement. So the performance review involves a second "sitting-down together" of boss and employee to discuss action plans and results, standards of performance and achievement, changes necessary in the vital result areas (because they can become obsolete), and the next set of improvement plans.

Benefits

With every new (or old) style of management there is always a temptation for the advocates to list the benefits and, rather like the desperate sellers of old-fashioned patent medicines, to list cures for all possible diseases so as to increase sales. All styles of management have their defenders; all styles have their good points, even if they are confined to "making the trains run on time." This is a modern and progressive style of management that has particular advantages in the field of marketing. These are threefold, though there may well be others that have been noted in different circumstances. They can be listed under the headings of *Investigation, Innovation* and *Motivation.*

Investigation

The *investigative* approach has been successfully introduced into companies where it has been generally carried through with the help of management consultants, who have found the technique hard to improve. It uncovers organizational defects at an early stage; brings into the open problems of relationships; and identifies not only the areas where improvements are necessary, but the ways in which they can be quickly accomplished.

Innovation

These days, many top managements demand a high level of *innovation* and creativity from their staff. Here also the philosophy assists. Innovation for its own sake is a fruitless exercise—a good way of losing money. If objectives are recognized and agreed on, then concentration on activities is lessened. More emphasis begins to be placed on results. In the writing up of job descriptions, even in the modern methods of job evaluation, the pressure is to list all the responsibilities that a job includes, all the activities that an employee performs. Try to pick out the five or six result-producing activities in which a real contribution to the company's profitability can be made.

Motivation

Finally, in the field of *motivation*, there are proven results in a number of companies. This approach avoids making people do the wrong things better. It helps middle managers meet the challenge of change. Even in the early stages of discussing with managers and salesmen what they thought were the real results of their efforts, a great upsurge of interest was evident in one company, along with a determination to develop better and more meaningful objectives. Performance reviews give a new opportunity for managers who can see their employees in outlying districts only two or three times a year to discuss real problems and not simply to go through the motions of a Royal Visit and an airing of complaints.

The greatest mistake that can be made is to believe that this is a panacea for all ills, or that it is a do-it-yourself kit for hard-pressed managers. But in the area of marketing it can certainly release new energies and can prepare companies for the future. To quote John Humble: "In helping existing managers to do a better job in line with company objectives, it creates the right kind of demanding environment in which tomorrow's managers can grow."

Management Guide Exercise

In order to familiarize yourself with the techniques (not to say the advantages), try the following exercise to assess your own tasks and performance standards.

1. In your present job you have various responsibilities and tasks. Among the many things you have to do and manage, which do you regard as the four or five key tasks that are fundamental to your job? In the terms that your team exists in order to contribute to the basic objectives of the business, these four or five tasks are your pay-off tasks, and the degree of success with which they are performed will depend on whether or not your team will in fact make the required contribution.

    Other activities can be seen as subordinate to these payoff tasks, being things done as a lead into or in support of the execution of a payoff task.
    Try to distinguish between these pay-off tasks and objectives. "To achieve sales targets" is an objective. What are the payoff tasks that contribute to achieving such objectives?

    List your payoff tasks in column one of your management guide.

2. Describe what you see as the required standards of performance for each of your payoff tasks. These standards are either a desirable situation or

an identifiable achievement, demonstrating that the task is being done as expected and required. There can be more than one standard of performance for each payoff task. (If you find it difficult to describe the required standards of performance for any particular task, think: "How would I describe what makes me appreciate that this task is not being carried out satisfactorily?" Then go on from there.)

List the standards of performance for each payoff task in column two of the management guide.

3. Describe for each standard of performance the means of control by which you measure job performance against that standard. The distinction here is between required performance (the standard) and the means by which you can measure whether the job is going as required (the control). Such controls may be in quantitative terms, such as sales returns, reports of frequency of occurrences, etc., or they may be in qualitative terms, by inspections, observations, or investigations. Both can be described.

   List these controls in column three of the management guide.

4. Against each key task and standard of performance list in column four the actions that need to be taken either to reach an agreed on standard or to improve the possibilities of reaching it—actions that can be taken by you, your boss, or others in the business.

5. Describe the main purpose of your job against which you can then test all the key tasks and standards of performance.

7

THE SKILL OF MANAGING TIME

Every manager complains at one time or another that he has insufficient time to accomplish all the things he wants to do, or, more important, all the things his boss wants him to do! Seminars are conducted, courses are given, books are written—all in an attempt to provide managers with the skill of managing time. Because time is a nonexpandable resource, that skill seems to be indispensable. In this chapter, some of the problems are discussed and some solutions are offered, in the hope that they may be of value, and in the certainty that all the aids to time control are essentially rooted in *self-discipline*.

Time Use

First, it is important to consider the use of time (that is, the time spent in the office doing business for which someone pays you) as being subject to two problem areas: time *wasted* and time *misused*. Time wasted is time we are personally responsible for and where we feel guilty wasting it. These feelings of guilt are aroused most easily when we suddenly realize that either we have been doing unnecessary things or, because of simple laziness, there is not enough time to complete an essential task. Tasks imposed by the boss are also sometimes considered to be time wasted!

Time misused, on the other hand, is caused by mistakes and faults in personal management style, by

- Doing too much, instead of "managing."
- Not delegating sufficiently to others who are competent to take the tasks that use up our own time.
- Lack of planning, a very human failing since everyone hates to make solid commitments about the future, which may turn out to be uninspired guesses or even disasters—preferring to be brilliant improvisers.
- Not establishing priorities in day-to-day needs, so that there is no way of deciding what should be done first and what can wait until later. (Airline reservation systems have a clever way of overcoming the seemingly overwhelming problem of chronological order. They have created the wait list. If the need to maximize the sale of higher paying seats takes preference over filling the aircraft, then it is impracticable to follow a purely chronological priority—first come, first served. There is a need to create a holding system or wait list, where the cheaper flier—and they usually apply first—can be stacked waiting for their fare level to be accepted.) To devise such a wait list system as a time control technique there is a need for an overriding factor other than first come, first served to determine priorities.

In an AMA Survey Report, "Executive Time Management," Philip Marvin, a professor at Cincinnati University, surveyed some 1,369 managers to discover how they used their time.[1] Professor Marvin notes that the manager's three roles—all of which are essential to getting things done—required an unexpectedly large amount of the manager's time. The roles were as follows:

- **Specialist** (doing what the manager was personally good at, e.g., selling, accounting, research)—**31 percent** of available time.
- **Managing** (planning, organizing, controlling)—**47 percent** of available time.
- **Mentoring** (showing others how to do things, helping to solve problems, evaluating performance)—**16 percent** of time.
- **Other activities—6 percent** of time.

At a recent seminar, a large group of managers was asked what *they* thought the breakdown ought to be. Their percentages were as follows:

- **Specialist—10 percent** of available time.
- **Managing—60 percent** of available time.
- **Mentoring—20 percent** of time.
- **Other—10 percent** of time.

They thought these were all reasonable targets to aim for.

If a manager is to meet these targets, however, he needs to acquire some skill in avoiding both time wasting and time misuse. There are two main techniques to accomplish this: the time log and time analysis.

Time Log

The time log is a list of activities shown as being performed within quarter-hour divisions of the office day. There are a number of copyright versions of the time log, but the simplest (that your secretary can create for you if you have no time!) is shown in Figure 7.1.

Each day is divided into quarter-hours and each activity is then described briefly—"opening mail," "drinking coffee." A manager once asked me what he should put in

	Date		
Time	*Activity*	*Cause*	*Remarks*
8:00 8:15		Me	
8:15 8:30		Me	
8:30 8:45		System	
8:45 9:00		Boss	
9:00 9:15			
9:15 9:30			
etc.			

Figure 7.1 Time Log

his time log when he had spent ten minutes looking out the window. I said that if he felt guilty about it he might put "strategic planning"; if not, "looking out the window." In either case it would make little difference to an *irretrievable* amount of time. Complications often arise in the next column: "Cause." Try to keep it simple and remember that there are only three forces operating on your time in the office: your self, the system, and your boss. In the system are included employees and peers, other office workers dropping by, business reps, accountants, and so forth. But there is no reason why you should not find all kinds of persons and circumstances that impose on your time. The "Remarks" column is for comments. It can be used to explain a special circumstance at a regular meeting or it can be used to note special needs, such as leaving early to attend a special event.

The time log should be kept by both you and your secretary (if you have a regular or permanent secretary, and it is a sign of the times, perhaps, that many executives do not, then that may be a good person to manage your time and to create the time log). But, as was mentioned earlier, most time management techniques involve self-discipline and, thus, it is probably best for you to keep your own time log, as it will enable you to make an objective analysis of where your time has gone and exactly who or what has imposed on you the different activities that have been logged.

The time log can help, first of all, by demonstrating *how long everything takes.* It also demonstrates how many things can perhaps be *eliminated*—the time wasters to start with, the unnecessary things like

- Doing the same job twice, because the whole matter was not thought through first.
- Being unwilling to start. It is quite amazing how many things there are that impede actually getting down to doing a particular task, like sharpening pencils, straightening the desk, reading the E-mail (just in case something there requires a totally different set of actions), and so on.
- Allowing interruptions. The time log will clearly demonstrate how many interruptions are allowed during the course of the day. One reason why many managers take work home is that in the home environment there is more control over interruptions.
- Daydreaming. This is not exactly necessary, but it is a time waster. The fact is that very few people are really able to concentrate hard on one subject for a long time. Listeners to a lecture are supposed to be able to concentrate for only about ten minutes at a

time. After that (and if you do not have this problem, skip this section), most people float off in a kind of dream, not necessarily a romantic type of daydreaming; simply another train of thought: what other work there is to do, should information for that report be collected now or later, is it possible to reorganize the filing system, sales force, and information system in one day...? Recognizing that mental concentration is limited, we should check on how we have used our time, and see what amounts or "chunks" of time we normally find acceptable. (There are those who find "bite-sized" chunks too small and have to take two at a time!)

Time Analysis

If the time log were simply to demonstrate how time is wasted, it would help enormously. But it can also help to analyze where the time has gone. If the analysis is carried some steps further than the simple "Cause" column on the time log, it can provide a basis for discussion with both bosses and employees.

Managers almost always need to discuss the extent of their job with their boss, and the changing priorities that are either being imposed upon them or that they are expected to impose. As discussed in Chapter 6, one of the most important (and pressing) manager needs is to get agreement from the boss as to what is expected: what are the dimensions of the job (the parameters), what are the standards of performance against which they will be judged, where does the company (in this case, the boss) want everyone to go this year (what are the objectives and strategies)? Even in enlightened companies, when this is clear, written down, and discussed, there always come moments of truth when the urgent takes precedence over the important and juniors have to set priorities which by rights belong to their seniors.

If time analysis can help to focus relationships with the boss, it can just as easily be used as the basis for discussions with employees. A major misuse of time is doing things that could (and should) be delegated to others. The definition of managing as "getting things done through other people" implies an ability and a willingness to delegate. The art of delegation involves knowing very clearly the extent of one's responsibility and trusting one's employee to be delegated the job, accepting full responsibility for the successful completion of the job by the employee, whether it is done right or wrong. It is another example of behavior changing attitudes. Just as long as you do not trust your employees to do something, you will think that they cannot. If you allow yourself to let your employees try, you will begin to change your attitude toward their ability to do a job.

Thus, before you delegate be sure to look carefully at how much your employees could do and discuss it with them; examine closely how much more responsibility could be delegated to secretaries or personal assistants; at what points in their operations do you have to make decisions, give approval, provide direction? What is their time span of discretion, i.e., how long can they work without supervision?

Having looked at the relationships with the boss and employees, there should be more time to think. But in order to make use of that time it is worth considering a number of time control techniques. These are not new, and are brought together here to use as instruments in making better use of time. They are called time control techniques as they are essentially controls on time use; they are not managing time, since it is an illusion that we can manage time. We can check where it is and how it is being used and certainly we can hope to improve its use.

Table 7.1 Checklist for Time-Control Techniques

1. *Set objectives.*
   If you know where you want to go, it saves a tremendous amount of time in trying to get there. It is amazing how many people do not think about objectives until after they are underway.
2. *Start a time diary.*
   Establish in advance how much time to set aside for each activity—reading the mail, attending meetings, writing reports, talking with staff, etc.
3. *Make a daily plan.*
   List at the beginning of each day (or even the night before) what you intend to do for the day. The list should be realistic in terms of what can be done that day.
4. *Establish priorities.*
   Look at what needs to be done (in numbers 2 and 3) and establish priorities in terms of importance or influence on results. Try putting the important before the urgent.
5. *Do one thing at a time.*
   Finish one job before beginning another. Time is almost always wasted restarting an activity, whether it is a piece of research, a letter to a client, or a proposal to a customer.
6. *Do difficult things first.*
   Some managers argue that it is easier to get the easy jobs out of the way before tackling the difficult tasks. Often doing the easy things first acts as a delaying tactic, so the harder work can be put off indefinitely—almost until it is too late.
7. *Use reminder lists and tickler files.*
   It is quite surprising how incorporating reminder lists or tickler files, which present in date order all the items that must be dealt with on a particular day, can save time and maintain priorities.
8. *Set deadlines.*
   Everyone postpones things until the last minute, especially difficult decisions or actions. Setting deadlines can help control the time needed for certain activities. It means that priorities can be set, that decisions are made, and that difficult problems are not forgotten until the last minute.
9. *Sort and review the mail.*
   Mail should be sorted, on receipt, into three stacks:
   - Immediate action. Add to time log for review.
   - Delegated (and controlled) action. Assign to appropriate employee for action.
   - Information (catalogs, etc.). Set aside for future action.

Table 7.1 Checklist for Time-Control Techniques (continued)

10. *Have agendas for meetings.*

    An agenda delineates specific topic for discussion, which reduces time spent talking about other subjects which have no relevance to the subject of the meeting.

    Following the meeting, action point minutes should be issued, such as this.

Subject	Discussion	Action
Time control	It was agreed that the agenda should be distributed at least two days in advance of the meeting.	AB (sec. JRC) before 4/3.

11. *Any other technique that you find practical and workable.*

8

WORKING IN GROUPS

Since the end of the Second World War, and partly because of it, a great deal of research has been done, and a great deal of experimentation has followed, into how groups work together. In many companies it has been seen that if committees and less formal groups of individuals can work effectively together there is more efficient decision making and operating. This clearly started from all the criticism that has been levelled in the past at committees: that a camel is a horse designed by a committee; that committees lack courage; that committees can never make decisions, and so on. For this reason a great deal of time and effort has been aimed at improving people's group performance.

Much of the trend toward sensitivity training which began to flourish in the early 1960s, was aimed at the fact that if people were to work successfully in a group (either of peers or of others of different status in an organization) a great deal more about individual strengths and weaknesses was needed. Whether this actually improved people's ability to work in groups has always been a matter of some doubt. What is true is that the effort involved in trying to see what makes groups tick has resulted in a great deal of information and knowledge.

But knowing what a person should do does not make him good at doing it. And this is why the manager needs some kind of framework or technique that he can apply both to himself and to his colleagues to make these groups work more efficiently.

A Model

Perhaps the simplest model is one that starts by stating

1. What our goal is.
2. What must be achieved to reach this goal.
3. How it is to be achieved.
4. The work to be performed.
5. The evaluation to see that the goals were achieved.

This sequence, which can apply to both individuals and groups, provides a framework against which the activity can be measured, monitored, controlled, and improved, or it can be scrapped and started again if necessary. Approached in more detail, it means that if group operations are involved it is absolutely essential to start by saying What are we trying to achieve?

As seen in Chapter 6, the first and most important aspect of the whole process and philosophy deals with the necessity of establishing goals. In operating in a group or a committee, whether formal or informal, whether haphazard, or ad hoc, whether in business or outside it, start by asking "What are the goals we intend to accomplish?" This is not only in terms of the committee's operation, but also in each individual meeting. What often occurs is that the meeting has an agenda, and the main objective is to try to get through the agenda. One of the basic problems is that we find that we are filling in time rather than reaching results.

Objectives

The definition of an objective is something that is to be accomplished or attained; it is where we want to arrive.

Clearly establish the goals to be achieved, otherwise, the whole activity of the group could get bogged down. Then establish what needs to be done to transform from the present to the goal; in other words, what needs to be done to achieve the results.

To reach an agreement on a particular course of action, assume that there is no agreement at the moment. To make a decision as to what should be done about a particular problem, this assumes that there is no decision at the moment. If simply exchanging views, then ensure that everybody's views are expressed and recorded. These are some of the tasks that must be carried out in order to reach the goal.

Resources

The next step is to plan how to distribute the resources in a way that allows those activities to be carried through. In the early stages the resources that are available in the group might not be known. All that is known is that there is a certain limited amount of time, there is knowledge, accumulated experience, and abilities to think through certain problems. Research has shown that group decisions tend to be, on average, better than individual decisions. It is only fair that the group function as efficiently and as effectively as possible. And in order to do that, identify all available resources.

The next step is actually doing what has been planned. This means that the group working needs to be carefully planned and supervised and everybody needs to understand what kinds of things happen when people get together to discuss a subject; when they come together in order to achieve a particular goal; when they unite in order to pool their knowledge, experience, and ability in order to achieve some kind of synergy.

And finally, in the model, there is a monitoring role, which is usually performed at the end of the group's activity. This feedback is necessary to improve the activity of the group the next time.

Beware of the "Abilene Paradox" (Harvey, 1989), which states that "people in groups tend to agree to courses of action which as individuals they know to be stupid."[1]

Influences on Behavior in Groups

The most important influence on behavior in the group comes from the personal characteristics of the individuals who form that group. These personal characteristics can be broken down into: personality, values, and abilities. For the most part these have to be taken as they stand; they can certainly not be changed in the short term. However, perhaps as important as inherent characteristics are two other influences on the individual: *physical influences* (air temperature, noise level, room size), and *social influences* (willingness or unwillingness to be thought a worthwhile member of the organization).

One of the most interesting discussions of the strength of social influences on the behavior of individuals began in the early 1970s with the publication of a paper by Allen and Pilnick, which described the way that norms (what people actually did, rather than what they thought they should do) affected the organization.[2]

Allen and Pilnick demonstrated that the power of the group was overwhelming in both positive and negative aspects of what people do. The most obvious effects—everyday norms—dress, speech, and interaction in a group, are strongly influenced by the work group or peer group to which we belong. People behave differently throughout the day, depending on the particular circumstances.

Fashions

Fashions are significantly illustrative of norms. Fashions and fashion-consciousness distinguish both men and women in terms of the group to which they belong. A new secretary who arrives without preconceived ideas in an office will very quickly adopt the dress norms of the staff already there. When joining an organization—a health club, a bridge club, or an amateur theatrical group—behavior patterns that do not appear in any rule book quickly develop.

A lot of norms have been found in organizations: not only dress and fashion, not only cultural and traditional, but norms specific to that organization—or to particular groups inside it.

Norms affect behavior in any group. Norms are among the first things learned when joining a group. Norms are the unspoken rules of behavior, and because they are unspoken, they are somehow also outside the individual. We do not behave in a particular way because we want to, but because "that's the way everyone behaves around here."

Consider the norms of punctuality in an organization. Apart from a few eccentrics, everyone in the group follows a similar approach to punctuality. People are generally punctual because it is the norm. In one company everyone arrives on time for work, but no one starts to work for half an hour or so. People chat about the evening before, or read the paper, or wander aimlessly from office to office. But then no one leaves promptly at five o'clock, because the "norm" is to work past "quitting time"—particularly if at the middle management level. This happens whether there is any work to be done or not.

Norms and Their Development

Norms develop in different ways. They can, of course, start by agreement among the original group. It is likely that this original agreement would get watered down over a period of time and other norms would take over. Norms can also start as a result of the behavior of a strong member of the group being taken as a model by the others. Resistance to authority usually starts this way, and the spread of information by means of the media helps. Every riot, every sit-in, every protest action, every flouting of authority is vividly presented in the media. When everyone can see the referee being challenged in professional football games, it is not surprising that this norm carries over to small boys playing football on Saturday afternoons.

In one company, the chief executive always worked in his shirt-sleeves. As a result, anyone who wanted to appear important also took his jacket off as soon as he arrived at the office. The idea was not to look important, but because it was the norm; the thing to do. Other norms in that company also originated from the behavior of the chief executive. His inability or unwillingness to delegate became a norm. His habit of cutting prices became a norm. All these norms arose because the behavior of the chief executive was taken as a model by other members of the group.

Rewarded Behavior

Other mainsprings of normative behavior come from the discovery, sometimes accidental, of a benefit from rewarded behavior. Conform with the group to be liked; to fit in; to have new friends. In one company, criticism was never given openly. It was not until after a meeting that those involved expressed their real views. Had they done so during the meeting itself much progress would have been made, but people would have been upset. It became the norm that comment and criticism were made in the staff lunchroom and in hallways—never during the meeting.

Research into norm patterns within companies revealed the fact that norms can be grouped together in defined clusters. For example, in most companies there is a whole cluster of norms around organizational pride. There are norms around performance and profitability, there are norms around supervision, there are norms around teamwork, and there are norms around training and planning.

In every organization people have views on certain matters, and if asked about training, for example, the view might be that an enormous amount of money is spent on training, but nobody gets promoted as a result of having been trained. Thus the views of training in that organization are fairly negative. However, a great deal of money is actually spent on the training process. Each of these clusters, therefore, has both positive and negative norms attached to it.

Changing Norms

The question can be asked: "What if the norms are identified—what can we do about them; can we change them? Is there some way to affect the normative behavior of the group?" There is—but it depends on awareness and understanding of norms. Once norms are understood it is easy to see them everywhere. Once identifiable, personal norms are clear, they can be laughed at. And then there is a choice! You can say: "Why am I doing this? Is there a better way?"

If you decide to introduce change into an organization—whether it is a golf club or a multinational corporation—first identify the norms. In the process of changing, everyone involved needs to be aware of the norms surrounding the group. Awareness brings with it the possibility of choice. Thus, as a group, changing the norms is most certainly possible.

Improving Efficiency

In trying to improve the efficiency of the group and its expertise in discussing matters, dealing with problems, and reaching solutions, it is essential to recognize that there are going to be norms in the group. It might be necessary to change those norms, so that the group can work toward the model that was demonstrated at the beginning of this chapter.

One way of doing this is by going through group exercises to establish how the group operates before getting down to serious work. There is a set of books published by Pfeiffer & Company called *A Handbook of Structured Experiences for Human Relations Training, Vol. I–X*.[3] The exercises in these books are concerned with group problem solving, demonstrating how a group goes about solving a relatively unimportant problem. There are exercises also that allow the group to look at its own reactions, exercises demonstrating how leadership arises within a group, and whether or not a leader is appointed; there are exercises that demonstrate the way in which, faced with ethical dilemmas, a group tackles these difficulties by creating its own norms, and there are exercises that demonstrate the difficulty of arriving at a consensus.

The last, a consensus problem, is typically one in which a number of items have to be put in a particular order: which profession is thought to be most important or have the best reputation, or which item of equipment is the most important for a particular project. Although in these exercises there is usually a "right" solution, the important aspect is whether the individual's priority list can be integrated into that of the group, and whether a consensus can be arrived at without too much disagreement. In the words of Mary Parker Follett: "Attempt an integration of views, rather than competition or cooperation." (Mary Parker Follett, *Creative Experience,* Longmans, 1924.)[4]

Group Types

In a book called *New Ways to Better Meetings,* B.W. and Frances Strauss have offered another way in which practice can assist in getting the group to work better.[5] Their first step shows that there are people in any group who need to be recognized: people who are basically either destructive or nuisances. (Generally, the positive group members do not demand recognition to the same extent.) Starting at the most negative end, they describe the *dominator,* the one who gives orders, dictates to the other members of the group, and usually picks on the weaker members to demonstrate his dictatorial powers; the *critic,* who criticizes others all the time, is sarcastic, and makes acid comments; and the *distractor,* who changes the subject, whispers to neighbors, and makes comments under his breath. These types are destructive simply because they want to be important.

Modified Versions

Here are several modified descriptions of group members as noted in the Strauss book.

- The *notetaker* has to note everything down and must get everything in the right order; everybody must wait while this is being done.
- The *clear definer* is unable to work unless the definition of what is being talked about is absolutely clear; who says: "Can we please define what we are talking about?"

- The *cynic* says: "It will never work, these things never do," or "We tried this before and it didn't work."
- The *superior person* is in the meeting by special invitation; he has all the answers, but will provide them only if everybody listens respectfully.
- The *fence sitter* only commits when it is clear which side will win.

Then there are three others whose participation in the group is often, in fact, welcome.

- The *talker* explains to anyone who will listen that he has a lot of experience in every facet of what is about to be discussed and goes on at length about that experience, relevant or not.
- The *enthusiast* gets very excited about every new idea.
- The *joker*, who seeks his importance in pointing out that there is an amusing story to be told about almost every subject, and almost every subject reminds him of one.

Organizing the Group

Recognizing that these types exist in most groups, it is necessary to practice so that the group's effectiveness can be improved. Most groups should have a leader and a recorder. In official committees this is the boss and his secretary. This probably means that the minutes of the meeting are highly biased in the direction in which the chairman would like them to be biased.

But, for a group to become more participative and to function as a group and not simply as a sounding board for the chairman's views, a much different collection of tasks must be distributed among a number of the members. There will still be a leader and a recorder, but these need not necessarily be the same people on each occasion. (However, in the early stages, these two should remain the same for purposes of training the group to become more effective.) The two others who are required in this process are a noteboard writer, who can record on the noteboard as the meeting progresses the various aspects of the subject being discussed—a list of advantages and disadvantages, possible courses of action, possible decisions, and lists of what the group has done.

And finally, for training purposes, there needs to be an observer who, in the initial stages says very little, but is careful to observe what the people in the group are actually doing. For purposes of improvement, there needs to be a postmeeting evaluation session where, at some point before the end of the meeting, the official subject is put aside and the members, with the assistance of the observer, discuss and evaluate what has happened. Videotaping the group is also an effective tool.

Interaction Score Sheet

Table 8.1 illustrates an interaction analysis score sheet, which can be used to assist the observer in making his analysis. On it there are twelve different descriptions of interventions by members of the group, A, B, C, D, and E across the horizontal axis. The different types of intervention are Accordance, Opinions, Questions, and Oppostition.

Accordance

Strongly agrees shown by saying "hear, hear" loudly, or slapping another person on the back, or giving a thumbs-up sign, or "tension release" shown by laughing, banging the table, or other ways of letting off steam. Or "agrees" shown by nodding or saying "I agree with that."

Opinions and Questions

The second and third categories, those on "Opinions" and "Questions," are the most popular—most successful groups have people who either ask questions or give opinions as a result of questions being asked of them. There are three types of opinions:

Suggestions: "I suggest that it should be like this"; the member concerned

Recommendations: "It is my recommendation that the whole idea direction should be something else";

Information: "You should know that this whole problem has been tackled two or three times before,"—which could be accurate or just an impression that might not be true.

The next section is, according to the Strauss team, the most helpful part of a membership of a committee or group. The member is *asking for information*, or *asking the views of* other members of the group, or *requesting ideas* from those members of the group. A number of typical questions that can fall into this category are shown.

Disagreement

Finally, the most destructive area is the area of *disagreement*. First is *straightforward disagreement* in the form of "definitely not," "absolutely wrong," "completely mistaken," "I disagree entirely with what has been said" or, going further into the emotional area, *showing tension*—swearing, eyes up to heaven, "What the blazes is going on?" "Whoever in his right mind...," "everybody must be mad," or even cynical loud laughter, sarcasm, and so on. And finally in this group is straightforward *antagonism;* emotional scenes like "I can't stand this," "I will have to leave," "I can't deal with this any longer," etc.

What the observer has to do is try to identify and categorize each of the responses by each member of the group. In the reaction discussion after the meeting, he can then emphasize that the most helpful comments were those

Table 8.1 Interaction Analysis Score Sheet

		\multicolumn{5}{c	}{*Members*}
		A	B	C	D	E
Accordance	1. Strongly agrees 2. Releases tension 3. Agrees					
Opinions	1. Suggests 2. Recommends 3. Informs					
Questions	1. Asks for information 2. Asks for views 3. Requests ideas					
Opposition	1. Disagrees 2. Shows tension 3. Antagonistic					

Strongly agrees: says "Go for it!," gives thumbs up. Releases tension: laughs, bangs the table. Agrees: I'll go along with that.
Suggests: I believe that it should be like this. Recommends: In my opinion there's a better direction! Informs: Did you know that this whole problem has been tackled two or three times before?
Asks for information: Does anybody know the exact requirements for this? Asks for views: What is your opinion of this solution? Requests ideas: How should the problem be tackled?
Disagrees: Definitely not! Absolutely wrong! Shows tension: Oh my God! What is going on here? Antagonistic: I can't stand this!

where questions were asked and that the most helpful areas of discussion were those that were begun by various people asking questions as to why something was as it was, rather than strong disagreement.

Summary

For a manager to improve his skills in dealing with groups and making them more efficient in their tasks, there are five things that he needs to do.

First, he needs to get agreement that there is a model of the behavior needed to get a result. This model is almost the same as the model for an individual, but this time it is necessary to get the group to agree that the model is important.

Second, he needs to recognize the enormous power of the group as an influence of behavior. This is not a new discovery, but nevertheless it has not been sufficiently investigated in the context of business situations, nor have its implications been fully recognized. It is also important to realize that once the group norms that prevail in a particular social unit have been identified, then there is the choice of either doing or not doing something about them. Once a group has recognized that the "local" norms which prevail are negative norms and can in the long run do harm both personally and professionally, they have a chance of doing something about them.

Third, it is important, if group work is to improve, that exercises be conducted to improve the way the group works together. Exercises should not only be done because they are enjoyable in themselves, but the post-exercise discussion is of great value in identifying the ways in which group behavior operates.

Fourth, he needs to recognize that there are a number of types who appear in almost all groups and have, in one way or another, to be coped with if the group is to perform successfully.

Fifth, reviewing a simple, analytical form used by an observer in the group can help him in analyzing how the group has behaved. It can provide him with a mirror that can help a group to improve its efficiency.

9

MANAGING COMMUNICATIONS

In a *Harvard Business Review* article in July 1952, the late Carl Rogers wrote "There is one main obstacle to communication: people's tendency to *evaluate*...[but]...if people can learn to *listen* with understanding they can greatly improve their communication with others." This chapter largely concerns these barriers and gateways to better communication.

Skill in communication is measured by the response the communication evokes: not only with what should be communicated but also how it should be communicated; not only what is said or written, but also what is heard, read, and understood. It is possible to improve communications by following some straightforward principles and recognizing the barriers that exist in the communication process. Effective communication that causes someone to do something is to a large extent dependent on efficient communication, which includes both the actual means of communication and the ways in which the communication is achieved. At the end of this chapter is a questionnaire that tests your personal communication skills.

What Should Be Communicated?

In most companies there are four main aspects of the business that should be communicated throughout the company so that the morale of the company is maintained and decisions are made that fit the company's image and style, not to say meet the company's objectives. The first aspect to be communicated is the company purpose—a description of the company's aims, the customers it serves, the products or services it intends to continue to provide, the interests of the different stakeholders (such as owners, managers, employees, and customers) and relations with government and other external organizations. As demonstrated in Chapter 1, this is the first step in company planning, and the process of arriving at an acceptable (and reasonably short) definition of company purpose is both time consuming and difficult. But it is the basis and foundation (as well as the yardstick against which measurements are made) of the major objectives and strategies of the company.

The second aspect that must be communicated to all levels of company personnel is the company's *long-range plan*, that is, the objectives and strategies in each of the company's key areas—those areas that are vital to the success and continuity of the plan. Objectives should be expressed in terms of what is to be maintained and what should be improved in each key area; strategies should be set out as the way in which objectives are to be achieved.

The third business aspect of the company is the *short-term plans*. If these are product plans, they should be communicated to all who are at present (or who are likely to be) involved in the plans, which include development, technical changes, quantities to be produced, attributes, factory output, packaging costs, and profitability. If they are marketing plans, they should include short-term objectives per customer per product, per period, promotion strategies and activities, selling goals and schedules of activity, service or technical backup, and cost allocations. They should be communicated in as much detail as possible to every one responsible for customer contact. One particular group that is often overlooked is the sales office or sales administration staff: those who deal with the paperwork of orders are often responsible for fielding customer inquiries and complaints, and may have responsibility for setting priorities. In short-term plans is included an item that also must be communicated—the *budget*—not only in terms of costs and revenues, but also to the background of these figures and the thought that has gone into the decision making.

Service industries need even clearer lines of communication, since the service only exists when the customer demands it. This implies that every single person who is likely to be in contact with the customer (or client) at any time needs to know company policies and needs to be empowered to use judgment when unexpected situations arise. Not only that, but staff need to be encouraged to report their experiences to all the other members of the business—to make communication "circular," so to speak.

Fourth, there is a need to disseminate *market information*. Chapter 2 describes the basis of a market information system and the kind of information that has to be collected. Trends in the market, forecasts of changes, both macro- and microeconomic, so that the input into decision making is of a higher standard, must be collected, collated, and communicated.

How to Communicate

The problems that arise with the physical aspects of communication are many, for although courses and seminars in public speaking usually have an enthusiastic audience there are still many areas where communication is inefficient, where the message does not get across, where the whole process becomes distorted through deliberate misunderstanding or careless underestimating of levels of intelligence.

There are four principles on which the different skills can be based, along with major barriers that need to be recognized.

The principles are

1. Decide what is to be communicated. What message are you trying to get across? What thought do you want to leave with the audience? What action do you want the listener to take? What level of information must be absorbed?
2. Identify who is to be communicated with (and if an ungrammatical sentence or phrase has more impact, use it!). All communication should fit the listener; it should fit his level of understanding. It is therefore vital to have a fairly clear idea with whom you are trying to communicate.
3. Arrange the communication as plain as possible. Simplicity is one of the hardest goals to achieve. Keep the message basic.
4. Ensure that the message is understood. Wherever possible, communication should be reinforced by some kind of feedback, to assure the sender that the message has been received.

Barriers to Reception

Whether the recipient is a listener or a reader, there are a number of barriers between the sending of emotional or cognitive data (i.e., information intended to affect opinions, attitudes or behavior, or information that is purely informative) and the reception, understanding, or acceptance of such data.

It has been demonstrated that at each stage in the communication process that there are barriers that must be overcome before the communication gets through to the recipient. For example, between the *sending* of a communication and its *reception* (or even perception) there are barriers such as the needs, anxieties, and expectations of the recipient and certain attitudes and values. This applies whether the recipient is listening to a lecture or reading the mail.

Barriers to Understanding

A second set of barriers, found between the *reception* of the message and the *understanding* of it are concerned with the ability of the recipient to concentrate on the communication (whether listening, reading, or watching), or with preconceived notions or open-mindedness and willingness to consider points of view and pieces of information that could upset ideas. (This is a point that is well understood by salesmen, and perhaps should be better appreciated by managers, especially those in marketing.) Of course there is a barrier that is connected with the recipient's existing knowledge. But perhaps most significant are the barriers created by the communicator in the length of the communication and the language in which it is couched. (This point is discussed later in the chapter.)

A third set of barriers is more difficult to penetrate, since it appears between the *understanding* of the communication and its *acceptance* by the recipient. These barriers include the attitudes and values of the reader or listener; these can lead to a clash of status between the sender of the message and the recipient. More difficult to avoid are the barriers created by the personal attributes of the sender—the gestures or mannerisms of a speaker, the use of unfamiliar language, inappropriate jokes, inaccuracies, etc.

Written Communication

It is important to recognize that effective written communication is only part of the total communication process.

Communication, after all, is the passing of an idea, fact, or some information from one mind to another. Although words are the easiest means of communication, the written word tends to have more weight than the spoken word, although there are a number of riders attached to this. If you can get people to listen to you, the spoken word has more weight; for example, if the speech, the documentary, play or television film engages the attention at the beginning. Nevertheless, in written communication as in any other form of communication (whether sending messages by beating drums or simply making faces at other people) the purpose of communication is to convey ideas. It is, therefore, to persuade, coax, cajole, arouse, stimulate, and finally to inform; the decisive element being what is heard, read, and understood.

Written communication, which is the normal day-to-day practice of a marketing manager, includes letters and reports, less often procedures and instructions, and occasionally writing direct mail and advertising copy. It is important, therefore, to say something about letters and reports and make some passing reference to the format of the others.

Writing Letters

There are a number of points to be made about the writing of letters. They should be written as if you were talking to the addressee; there should be no complicated jargon and the style should suit your relationship to the recipient. Even in the opening salutation there is a difference between "Dear Joe," "Dear Mr. Smith," "Dear Smith" or "Hello."

The development of this style is extremely difficult if dictating letters either into a dictating machine or to a secretary; there is no general overview of the kind of style that is being built up until the letter has been typed. Then the temptation is, because it looks impressive, to send it to the addressee without any changes. In the dictation of a long letter, words and phrases that are normal when we are talking to somebody sound rather long-winded when written in a letter. Dictating, therefore, requires not only careful discipline in its initiation, but also considerable attention in checking that what has been dictated reads well in its letter form.

The purpose of a letter must also be kept in mind throughout the writing or dictating and the checking process. It may well be written to maintain a relationship, to convey information, or to persuade a recipient of something—if only of the goodwill of the writer.

It must also be remembered that letters convey not only *meaning* but *tone*. In that regard, they must therefore be easy to read in terms of layout, format, and sentence and paragraph length. There is also a difference between letters originated by the writer and those that are sent in reply to a request from someone else. Two rules regarding tone are offered in *The Complete Plain Words* by Sir Ernest Gowers: First, "Be sure that you know what your correspondent is asking before you begin to answer him. We should try always to put ourselves in the position of the correspondent," and the last, "Use words with precise meanings, you have no business to leave your reader guessing."[1]

Writing Reports

Writing industrial reports is entirely different and requires different skills. In general, industrial reports are concerned with recording work done, assessing the situation, indicating a course of action to be taken, or keeping others informed of work that has been done. Therefore, their purpose can be seen to be to supply the reader with information he needs in order to understand what has been done or is to be done, in a form that he can understand. A report can be an important basis for a group concerned with a project's progress.

There are a number of fallacies about industrial reports. One is that the writer likes writing them and the reader likes reading them. Another is that size as such is impressive, and that if enough facts are put into the report the reader will sort them out for himself. Finally, and perhaps worst of all, is the fallacy that a report requires special jargon.

The skill of report writing is not so much in the style of the language that is used but in the way in which the report is prepared and put together.

Questions

There are three vital questions which the industrial report writer needs to ask before starting.

- What is the subject of the report?
- What is the purpose of the report?
- Who will read the report?

Answering the first question requires a certain amount of thought: Are the terms of reference available, and if they are not, what can be done about it? The terms of reference, after all, define the scope of the report and the lines the writer is required to follow. If they are followed, the report writer can avoid irrelevancies and distracting side channels. If no terms of reference have been given, he should put them together himself. If the terms of reference are not clear, he needs to clarify them. He should in any case establish, perhaps in one line, the basic objective of the report he is about to write.

The second question—the report's purpose—can also be difficult to answer. The report may be written to record events that have occurred; it may be necessary to write a report to describe facts; it may be necessary to make recommendations, or (and many reports have this as a hidden purpose) it may be written to persuade the reader to a course of action. (Many market research reports are written to persuade the reluctant marketing manager to a course of action that the market research staff believes is absolutely necessary and that is perhaps not adequately demonstrated by the bare statistics.)

The third question—to whom is it to be addressed—is also vital, as it is with letters and other forms of communication. There is a possibility that the writer knows the reader; in that case he can take into account other facts, such as whether the reader looks at every word or skips to the main argument; whether he simply wants the recommendation and does not want to read all the back-up documentation and information or—and this is much more often true than is usually recognized—whether he knows the answer already and simply wants to use the report to convince a particular person. This is very often true of consultant reports that are written for clients, which are used by clients as political weapons.

Report Framework

Two other points are worthy of note in the skills of report writing: first, how the report outline should look, since this is an important stage of preparation, and second, some of the ways in which facts can be collected.

The report framework should be as follows:

- Introduction (terms of reference; outline of the report)
- Findings
- Inferences (assumptions)
- Recommendations
- Results expected

- Action needed
- Conclusions
- Appendices

Some report writers tend to start out with a framework of this kind, then fill in each of the sections with the appropriate subheadings until finally they have sufficient information and sufficient material to create the report. Others start by discussing and writing out the *recommendations* and the *results expected*, then perhaps work back into the writing of *findings* and *inferences*.

However the report outline is put together, the stage of fact collection is a vital part of report writing. If this is not done thoroughly, no matter how carefully the report is written, or how good it looks, the effect is not going to be as great as when the facts are thoroughly researched.

In collecting facts it is important to first establish what sort of facts need to be collected. For most reports it is useful to use the heuristic method—a trial-and-error or discovery strategy. Thus in order to establish what sort of facts should be collected it is usually necessary to start out with some sort of hypothesis.

Fact Collection

A number of other points need to be made about the collection of facts, since there are perhaps four major sources of information:

1. Personal observation (a dangerous and probably a last-resort source of information).
2. The printed word (books, articles and documentation).
3. Visual media (films for example).
4. Personal interviewing (talking to the people who were there).

In collecting facts, clearly the accuracy of those facts will at some stage have to be checked, which means that the sources of information will need to be noted and will need to be very reliable. Notes will need to be made of facts, they will need to be indexed, and their sources will need to be carefully checked.

In personal interviewing it is essential to prepare the subject matter and the questions that are to be asked of the interviewee. Do not be distracted by listening to what the interviewee wants to talk about—ask for only the facts that you want to extract. It is very often worthwhile to play back the questions and answers to the interviewee to ensure that the information is accurate and acceptable. Finally, in any interview, always keep your options open to go back and ask further questions or to check that the answers you have received are correct. Here now is the foundation for a report.

Language

At this point it is suggested that Sir Ernest Gowers *The Complete Plain Words* be followed in terms of language. In particular, his advice that one should:

> "use no more words than are necessary to express your meaning,"
> "use familiar words rather than far fetched words," and
> "use words with a precise meaning rather than those that are vague."[2]

All writers of reports or letters should have synonyms for words like "develop," "involve," "major," and "overall." In *Plain Words*, "involve" has fourteen synonyms shown in the text, "overall" has twelve. It is all too easy to use words like "situation" instead of thinking out a more specific word to describe what is happening. Avoid getting "immersed in a concrete situation."

With regard to punctuation, Mark Twain is said to have written a note to his publisher saying "scatter colons, commas, and dashes at will." This is perhaps an exaggerated approach to the importance of punctuation; it is important to put in stops to help your reader to understand you. But too much punctuation is almost as bad as too little. Short sentences in a narrow column of a newspaper are far more acceptable than in the wider columns of a book or the even wider columns of A4 report paper.

Do not start to write a report until you have (a) created a framework, (b) filled it out with subsidiary facts and a conclusion, and (c) completed all fact finding. Then write first the body of the report, the facts and conclusions, then the recommendations, and finally the introduction and conclusion. Table 9.1 gives a brief checklist on layout and content.

(A subsidiary note on rewriting. It takes a considerable effort of will to rewrite a piece that has taken a lot of time and effort. Nevertheless, any report that is important, that may be required to be a selling document, or that is a vital aid to reaching a decision should be read and edited by a second person. The task of such a second opinion is not to rewrite the report but to assess whether the recipient will react as required; to suggest changes, additions, deletions, inconsistencies of style, etc., and to recommend perhaps a rearrangement of the argument. The principle is that the editor is more objective and can therefore make helpful suggestions in areas where the writer can no longer see clearly.)

Making Presentations

Managers, and particularly marketing managers, are expected to make presentations of different types during the course of the year. This may include dinners, shareholders' meetings, and possibly conferences; certainly business presentations to customers, distributors, and agents of new

Table 9.1 Layout and Content of the Report

1. *Introduction*
   What the report is about, who asked for it, and an outline of the various parts. This should also include some details of the amount of work that has been put into it.

2. *Facts*
   The only facts that should be included are those from which inferences, conclusions, or recommendations may be drawn. The first thing to do, therefore, is to put the facts in order, i.e., list the appendices in logical order.

3. *Inferences or Implications*
   The importance of these depends entirely on who is reading the report. Identify significant facts — variances from norms, changes over the years, trends in situations, etc.

   Highlight points where recommendations will be made. In the case of facts that the reader is likely already to know, put in a disclaimer such as "For completeness," because the reader may not know *all* the facts. Finally, check the logic of the conclusions that have been drawn from the facts. Can they be seen to follow?

   Do not introduce anything new at this stage.

4. *Conclusions/Recommendations*
   To make it easier to read the report, consider using the format
       fact—conclusion
       fact—conclusion
       fact—conclusion

   Each point must, however, be clearly separated and conclusions must be (a) consistent with facts, (b) reasonable and logical, (c) clear, and (d) concise (perhaps itemized). Whatever you do, do not manipulate the facts.

   Recommendations: what needs to be done as a result of the information or facts that have been presented. Recommendations need thoughtful judgment before they are made. Do not rush into making recommendations that seem to follow from the facts without taking into account the feelings of the reader. Thus recommendations should not only be sound and well defined but also discreet (taking into account the feelings of those involved) and, finally, fully considered including all the possible consequences.

5. *Appendices*
   The facts presented in their entirety.
   - Graphs—with a zero point on both axes.
   - Statistical information, remembering that pictures are often much easier to understand than columns of figures.
   - Results of experiments.
   - Maps, charts, and diagrams.

   It has been said that if the appendices are right the report will write itself.

products and new policies, new advertising messages, and new ideas; probably sales presentations to groups and committees; often, reports to colleagues.

There are considerable differences between these types of presentation. Speeches depend for their success more on public speaking skill and ability; business presentations depend on the ability of the presenter to assemble a collection of different aspects of the subject in order to persuade his audience in the manner of an advocate rather than a lecturer; selling to groups makes use of selling skills; reporting to colleagues is usually done against a very critical background. Successfully communicating to all these different groups always requires careful planning and preparation.

Presentation Preparation

This includes

1. *Setting objectives.* Ask (again!) what is the result to be achieved. Should the audience depart ready to take action, having gained more knowledge?
2. *Identifying the audience.* Nothing is more frustrating both to the audience and the presenter than a presentation that takes no account of the level of the audience, the types of people, and their previous experience and expectations. It is important to realize that the audience will give the presenter the benefit of the doubt up to a point.
3. *Establishing the structure of the presentation.* This means putting together an outline of the subject, and then deciding if more than one speaker is needed, if visual aids are to be used, etc.

    To establish the structure of a presentation, it is a good idea to look at the subject horizontally rather than vertically as shown in Figure 9.1.

```
                    Subject (Including Objectives)
    ┌───────────────┬───────────────┬───────────────┬───────────────┐
                        Present        How These        Future
    History             Problems       Were Tackled     Action
    A (V)               A              A (V)            A (V)
    B                   B (V)          B                B
    C (V)               C              C (V)            C (V)
    D                   D (V)          D                D (V)
                        E
```

Figure 9.1 Presentation Structure

Then each aspect can receive a V for vital, together with a speaker's name, and any other kinds of information as to how it might be included in the total presentation (by means of 35 mm slides, a film, a lecture, a discussion, and so on).

4. *Making estimates of times.* Most presenters feel that there is too little information with which to fill the time available. In fact it is usually the opposite: There is too little time to get across all the ideas that *must* be presented. It is important to remember the difficulty of holding the full attention of the audience for more than about ten minutes at a time, and breaks are necessary about every forty minutes. Thus, introductions and conclusions should take no longer than ten minutes each, and the other parts of the presentation should be designed in segments of thirty to forty minutes. It will soon be discovered that no audience ever complains about ending a few minutes early!

5. *Selecting and briefing speakers.* The selection of speakers and the programming of their participation is

extremely important. It needs to take into account the following characteristics:

- Knowledge of the subject.
- Experience in talking about it.
- Experience in public speaking.

The briefing should ensure that all speakers understand:

- The objectives of the presentation.
- Their role in the whole program.
- When, where, and times of run-throughs, etc.

Two other important points need to be made about presentations, the first with the presenter himself, and the second with visual aids.

The presenter has to be aware of the barriers to communication mentioned earlier in the chapter. In order to overcome them, perhaps he should start by looking at a checklist on public speaking (included in the reference section of local bookstores). This will provide a basis for

- Planning and establishing objectives, design structure, etc.;
- Preparing by writing out the talk, then writing it to be read, then condensing it to paragraph headings and perhaps notes on cards;
- Arranging material in a *logical* order, but presenting it in a *psychological* order; in terms of impact;
- Rehearsing, using closed circuit television if available or simply presenting it to a coworker. Do not underestimate the importance of rehearsal—it can make all the difference between success and failure, between acceptability and excellence.

Visual Aids

The purpose of visual aids is to appeal to another sense, and thus to increase the probability that the listeners will retain the information given. The use of such aids in these days becomes essential if the audience's interest is to be maintained—"one picture is worth a thousand words" it is said—in these days because most listeners are used to the supreme audiovisual medium, television.

There are, however, two types of visual aid, which have different usage patterns: the preprepared visual aid and that created during the session. In the first category are slides, films, videotapes, and prepared transparencies for the overhead projector. In the second come flipcharts, the noteboard and the transparent plastic sheet or roll and marker for use with the overhead projector.

As was said earlier, preparation is the secret of good presentations. The noteboard and flipchart should be used only sparingly, therefore. The transparent plastic sheet on the overhead projector has distinct advantages, in that it allows the lecturer to face the audience while drawing or writing on the sheet. The flipchart has the advantage of semipermanence, in that what is written on it can be retained (attached to a wall in the lecture room) for future reference.

Films and slides have the advantage of professionalism, and can show photographs of real events, whereas transparencies are very expensive when reproducing photographs. Slides can also show close-ups of machinery or events, human expression, etc., which may be important. They should be used where their strengths are evident. Videotapes, when used, should also present information, sketches of situations, for example, which cannot be shown or explained with words or diagrams. (A recent videotape was shown of a lecture given by a well-known lecturer with a blackboard—which was much less interesting than the man in person would have been!)

Films should have a close relationship to the subject matter, even if showing it from a different angle. Films should be used as part of a presentation or as the center of a discussion. Slides are an impressive backup for presentations and straight lectures. (Discussion is inhibited by the need for a darkened room, so the presenter should be lit by a spotlight.) Illustration, however, of places, systems, or machines is best done with slides, which can be changed at any speed the presenter selects.

Preprepared transparencies for the overhead projector are the most flexible aid in common use. They can be produced with specially designed script or typescript, handwritten, or created by using graphics packages on personal computers. They can be used to summarize, outline, or illustrate, or to reinforce ideas, concepts, and principles. The overhead projector does not require a darkened room, thus the slides can be used as the basis of a discussion. They can be added to by using the plastic roll on the projector or by using a modem directly connected to a computer so that what appears on the computer's visual display also appears on the overhead projector's screen.

Communication Instruments

There are four major instruments available by which communications can pass in any direction from one part of a company to another. (Communications with customers are usually part of sales and advertising policy—they are not within the subject matter of this book.)

    1. *Committees* have been mentioned in Chapter 8 in connection with the effort to improve effectiveness in achieving results. One committee that has a useful

part to play in the communications network of the company is the planning committee, and in the context of this book, the marketing planning committee. A planning committee has the advantage that everyone on the committee is aware of what is being discussed; it preempts the need for a further and parallel communication stream. But there are disadvantages: No one feels responsible for the recommendations that are made or for the final result that comes from the committee's labors. And a committee, in most profit-making companies, is unable to take action; there is rarely a situation in such organizations where a committee has authority in its own right.

2. *Reports* are often used as a communications medium. Many worldwide companies have a careful pattern of reporting, constructed along the lines given earlier in this chapter. A major problem is that local circumstances tend to overwhelm even the best written report. It is important to always have a kind of response factor built in, so that the reader must reply and demonstrate that he has noted the content of the report.

3. Regular *meetings*, (whether weekly or monthly), are perhaps the best means of communication in an organization. To ensure that full advantage is taken of this activity, they need careful preparation: Time should be taken in putting together the agenda, and the minutes of the meeting which follow should have a column that identifies the person responsible for particular action and the date when the action is to be reviewed. Simply adding this to the minutes of *all* meetings often has a remarkable impact on their effectiveness.

4. The *managerial chain* described by Rosemary Stewart in her book *The Reality of Management* is both upward and downward, and its importance is underrated by those managers who spend too much of their time doing rather than managing (see Chapter 7 in this book on managing time). Rosemary Stewart produces her own list of barriers to communication occurring in the organization, which resembles the barriers mentioned earlier in this chapter, adding two or three which are of particular relevance. In *downward* communication she includes the difficulty for a subordinate of distinguishing between advice and information and orders; which means that the manager needs to be careful about tone and wording when truly giving "advice." *Upward* communication has a barrier in the belief of managers that "my door is always open." In practice this means that, in an autocratically run company, no one wants to be seen talking to the boss, and in a participatively run company, the boss never gets any time to himself. An always-open door is, perhaps, an even greater barrier to communication than a closed one. *Sideways* communication is interrupted by such barriers as jealousy, willful misunderstanding, and unwillingness to take responsibility.[3] (The inventory that follows the next section illustrates how readers see the people around them and how barriers may be broken down.)

Communication With Outside Contractors

Many more businesses in the 1990s will either be contracting out some of their functions or become contractors for larger organizations or businesses. In the relationship between contractor and client, good communication is very important.

For the marketing manager (or the owner of a small business who is managing his own marketing), contracting out will normally involve agencies that undertake market research, PR agencies, or advertising and sales promotion agencies. Occasionally product development consultants and direct marketing agencies could be used.

Communication with such contractors will involve three major subjects:

- Satisfactory briefing as to the requirements of the marketing manager (or proprietor).
- Continual checks on the quality of the work being done.
- Regular reviews of briefing, results, and relationships.

For the briefing to be satisfactory, there is a need for a written brief, covering the objectives of the work to be done, the resources that will be assigned to the job, dates of review and completion, and agreed-on costs. The brief would result from a series of meetings and the consideration of several drafts.

Checks on quality would initially follow the lines laid down in the brief. (Too many of those who contract out seem to think that the threat of not renewing the contract is sufficient motivation for the contractor to maintain standards.) A report could be asked for, or a planned meeting held with a fixed agenda.

Both the client and the contractor would be anxious to straighten out any slippage or variance issues.

Regular reviews of the results (which would include discussion of the original brief) and relationships would take the form of a report followed by a meeting between the principals of both client and contractor. The heads of discussion would be the same as appeared in the original brief.

It is worth noting that in contracting out, communication plays a crucial role in motivating the contractor. Good communication is indeed far more effective than money or threats.

Inventory of Communication Tools

The final section of this chapter is an inventory of communication activities, skills, and responsibilities. Use this to evaluate specific communication requirements.

Confidential Self-Evaluation Inventory

There is no assumption that this inventory covers everything about a manager's communication activities, skills, and responsibilities. It is intended merely as a sampling of ideas and points of view that are well supported by contemporary research and authoritative opinion. No particular manager, supervisor, or executive is implied in the items that follow; rather a generalized or typical manager is assumed. (Obviously, no two individuals should be expected to behave in identical ways—people are different and situations are different.)

Respond to these questions as thoughtfully and as frankly as possible. Keep this inventory as a reminder that you can review now and then.

Score yourself on each item by circling *one* of the four numbers in the right-hand column. Interpret the numbers as follows:

4—I do this exceptionally well. (Outstanding)
3—I am basically all right here, although there is room for improvement. (Satisfactory)
2—Fair; sometimes I am all right, sometimes not; I should definitely be concerned. (Fair)
1—I need to work hard on this; there is room for significant improvement. (Needs work)

(In all cases, a yes answer is considered the proper answer—based on currently available research evidence and authoritative opinion.)

1. There is a general atmosphere of openness, that is, there are very few secrets, and it is easy for people to find out what is really going on.

4   3   2   1

2. I encourage an atmosphere of candor and frankness, so that people feel free to speak their minds.

       4   3   2   1

3. I have created conditions in my area of responsibility that encourage people to get together informally to discuss problems and new ideas.

       4   3   2   1

4. All of my associates (including all employees) are familiar with all the basic policies and procedures that have a bearing on their work; they have easy access to policy statements and rules. (There are no secret policies.)

       4   3   2   1

5. The communication lines are well known; people know to whom they report, whom they should see for specific information, where to find any answers, etc.

       4   3   2   1

6. Whenever I make (or participate in) an important decision, I consciously take into consideration such issues as
   (a) Who should participate in this decision (in terms of contributions to make, involvement, etc.)
   (b) How the decision should be communicated (i.e., when, by whom, to whom, in what order)

       4   3   2   1

7. I avoid assuming that top management has all the answers or all the wisdom; therefore, I avoid talking down to employees, or preaching to them—especially on such subjects as politics, free enterprise, and unions. (This

does not mean, however, that I am nervous about taking candid, forthright positions when the situation requires it.)

        4   3   2   1

8. In general, I have trust and confidence in my superiors; and so far as I can estimate, my employees have trust and confidence in me; i.e., there are no serious credibility gaps.

        4   3   2   1

9. I create a climate in which backstabbing or destructive win-lose conflict is avoided—especially between or among equals.

        4   3   2   1

10. I encourage widespread sharing in the discussion of goals and the setting of standards.

        4   3   2   1

11. I have seen to it that, within the limits of my power and responsibility, there is a clear and specific system of information exchange; decision centers and action centers have been identified and they receive the information they need when they need it.

        4   3   2   1

12. People have a clear understanding of what is expected of them on the job, and they have periodic opportunities to discuss their performance with superiors; these discussions are characterized by a free two-way exchange of views (rather than a lecture from the superior).

        4   3   2   1

13. I encourage the use of informal chain of command conferences, in which policies and problems discussed at higher levels are quickly interpreted and passed down the line, and in which ideas from below can be passed up the line.

    4   3   2   1

14. I encourage various systems and methods designed to tap the thinking of employees (i.e., to get feedback input), so that I can be informed of people's problems and feelings.

    4   3   2   1

15. I strive to give feedback in the form of prompt and meaningful answers to questions, suggestions, and complaints from below.

    4   3   2   1

16. I am readily accessible to anyone who wants to talk to me.

    4   3   2   1

17. I encourage true problem-solving conferences, where group decisions are honestly and thoughtfully discussed, free from manipulative pressures from the boss.

    4   3   2   1

18. When I conduct meetings, I see to it that they start and end on time and that (when appropriate) clear agendas are circulated to all parties in advance, with a relaxed atmosphere that allows people to speak up.

    4   3   2   1

19. I encourage participation—in various ways and degrees—of all those people who have something to

contribute to a decision (regardless of their rank or position).

    4   3   2   1

20. When it is necessary to announce important changes, I make every effort to indicate clearly the reasons why the changes are being made. I am especially careful that the people most directly involved are notified—early and privately, preferably face to face.

    4   3   2   1

21. I try to keep an open mind when suggestions, ideas, and proposals for new ways of doing things are offered (regardless of the source), and I avoid jumping in with criticism before the idea has been fully aired; I am able to tolerate a considerable amount of argument and dissent.

    4   3   2   1

22. In listening and in speaking, I avoid the trap of assuming that everything is only black or white; I avoid flat, dogmatic generalizations about human beings and human affairs *(without* being wishy-washy on honest convictions based on good evidence and careful thinking).

    4   3   2   1

23. I encourage the use of informal, personalized, face-to-face communication whenever conditions permit, especially when dealing with sensitive or complicated matters.

    4   3   2   1

24. I am suspicious of the old adage, "Don't say it—write it." I avoid ruling by written directives and memoranda.

    4   3   2   1

25. When dealing with employees and peers, I listen more than talk; ask questions rather than make pronouncements.

          4   **3**   **2**   **1**

To find your score, add up all the numbers you have circled, which will tell you your percentage. Then, consider these conclusions.

    (a) Any total score over 80—very good, overall.

    (b) Scores between 70 and 79—not bad, but cause for concern.

    (c) Scores below 70—danger!

Regardless of your total score, give careful thought to any twos circled, and start thinking about a crash program for any ones circled!

    Think about how your associates or employees would score you.

III

Skills Involved in Controlling Marketing

10

MARKETING MANAGER'S PROFIT RESPONSIBILITIES

In this section of the book are explanations of some of the more common problems the marketing manager is faced with when he is trying to discuss financial and accounting matters with the accountant, and when he himself is being asked by the chief executive to justify marketing expenditure.

To demonstrate the profit responsibilities of the marketing manager it is worth repeating that the aim of marketing is to obtain the maximum number of favorable buying decisions, and that this aim involves costs that must be controlled. Before discussing the aspects of costs (and cost centers) and profits (and profit centers), it would be valuable to reiterate one or two items of basic accounting items, so that, as a member of the management team, the entire marketing staff knows what everyone is discussing.

Financial Statements

There are two basic financial statements that are produced either because the law says they must be or because the business needs them in order to respond to controls. The first is the *balance sheet,* a picture of the financial condition of a business at a particular point in time (half-year, quarter, etc.) This statement balances liabilities and assets, as shown in Figure 10.1.

Liabilities and Shareholders' Equity	Against	Assets
Share capital		Fixed assets at cost
Reserves		(Less depreciation)
Retained profits		Land, buildings,
Long-term liabilities		plant, machinery
(Loans, etc.)		
Current Liabilities		*Current Assets*
Creditors		Cash
Taxation		Debtors
		Stocks

Figure 10.1   Balance Sheet

The second financial statement is the *profit and loss statement*, as shown in Figure 10.2.

The profit and loss statement gives a picture of the results of the firm's operations over a certain period. It can be drawn up monthly or quarterly—it is always drawn up annually.

The generally accepted objectives of accounting are the periodic measurement and statement of capital and income, and the provision of means of control by management. (The last often gets stamped by the first, since the first is also often a legal requirement.) There are major principles on which accounting within a business enterprise is constructed. It is important that the users of accounting information be aware of these principles, so that any misunderstanding can be avoided.

1. For accounting purposes an enterprise is assumed to be an accounting unit—separate from its owners (business as an entity).
2. Accounts that record acquisition of assets and liabilities are *capital* accounts (such as the balance sheet). Accounts that measure increase or decrease in capital are *revenue* accounts, which means that for every

XYZ Company
Profit and Loss Statement
for the Year Ended May 19—

		$
Sales		500,000
Less cost of goods sold*		300,000
Gross profit		200,000
Less expenses		
Warehousing	15,000	
Distribution	20,000	
Selling	30,000	
Advertising	50,000	
Administration	25,000	
		140,000
Operating profit		60,000
Less nontrading items		5,000
Profit before tax		55,000
Tax provision		26,400
Net profit after tax		28,600

*Cost of goods sold is arrived at by the computation shown in Figure 10.3.

Figure 10.2 Profit and Loss Statement

transaction the choice must be made between capital and revenue accounts. Managers need analyses of transactions that have caused increases or decreases in capital, summarized in the form of a profit and loss account. This merely measures the value of additions to capital in the form of sales and other income, and the losses of capital in the form of the cost of goods sold and selling and administrative expenses (distinction between capital and revenue).

3. The double-entry principle is, in essence, that every transaction is entered twice in the accounts. For example, if additional funds are brought into the business (e.g., an issue of more shares) this has two

	Cost of Goods Sold	
Expenditure chargeable to the factory		$
(1) Direct costs		
Raw materials	60,000	
Purchased parts	20,000	
Wages of factory workers	80,000	
Total direct		160,000
Indirect (overhead) costs		
Factory supervision	40,000	
Indirect labor	30,000	
Supplies	15,000	
Other services	55,000	
Depreciation of plant	60,000	
Total indirect		200,000
Total costs of production		360,000
(2) Work in process at beginning		60,000
Costs of production (as above)		360,000
		420,000
Less work in process at end		40,000
Value added to finished goods		380,000
(3) Value of finished goods at beginning		900,000
Value added to finished goods		380,000
		1,280,000
Less value of finished stock at end		980,000
Costs of goods sold		300,000

Figure 10.3 Computation of Cost of Goods Sold

effects: It increases the *liabilities* of the business to the owners, and it increases the *assets* of the company.

4. The financial statements of a business are prepared on the assumption that it is a going concern. This continuity assumption is that the business will not be sold or liquidated in the near future, but will continue to carry on toward its operational goals indefinitely. The consequence of this is that the current estimated fair-market value or prices of assets such as land, buildings, and plant *that will not be sold* are of no particular importance. In the balance

	Product Group X	
		$
Revenue		60,000
Manufacturing costs of units sold		35,000
Direct costs		
Salesmen	3,000	
Transport	1,500	
Warehousing	1,200	
Commission	1,500	7,200
Fixed costs (allocatable)		
Advertising	1,500	
Sales promotion	250	
		1,750
Fixed costs (apportioned)		
Administration (10% of sales)	6,000	
General overhead (5% of sales)	3,000	
		9,000
	Net profit	7,050

Figure 10.4 Full-Cost Allocation Report

sheet (Figure 10.1), such assets are shown at cost less depreciation (going concern principle).

5. Revenue is defined as "the considerations received for the aggregate of products and services transferred by an entity to its customers." Under this principle, revenue is realized when title to the goods sold transfers and when services are rendered. There is a further principle that can cause confusion to marketing managers. This states that, for each period, the revenues of the period must be identified and recognized in the accounting process. Then all of the costs incurred in generating that revenue, irrespective of the period in which the costs were incurred, must be identified with the period in which the revenues are recognized (matching principle). This principle requires the accrual and deferral of

many costs, but it causes confusion when it is applied to difficult accounts such as advertising costs or research and development costs, whose allocation to particular revenues is a matter of informed judgment.

Marketing and Selling Costs and Contribution

Marketing and selling costs are often lumped together as overhead, partly for convenience and partly because it is difficult to follow the matching principle. (Not only do advertising and selling costs for a given period not necessarily generate revenue in that same period, but it is often difficult to say when they *do* generate revenue.) If (rightly) marketing departments are to be held accountable for the activities of marketing, then the persons and responsibilities must be defined and accounting data produced matching the responsibilities.

Cost centers (the smallest segment of activity for which costs are accumulated) and Profit centers (business segments responsible for income and cost, but also for relating income to its invested capital) should be identified. Profit centers must also have the ability to choose both supply sources and output customers; trying to create them without those freedoms will mean that they will not work. The marketing manager has profit responsibilities because he: (a) has control over cost and revenue and return on invested capital (see ROI in Figure 10.6), (b) is responsible for pricing the products and forecasting the revenue, and (c) must allocate resources to meet contribution objectives. (See Table 5.1 on page 97—contribution being defined as the difference between direct costs and revenue.)

In contribution accounting, the report (Figure 10.5) excludes those costs that cannot logically be charged to the

	Product Group X	
		$
Revenue		60,000
Costs of goods sold		35,000
Direct costs		
Salesmen	3,000	
Transport	1,500	
Warehousing	1,200	
Commission	1,500	7,200
Fixed costs (allocatable)		
Advertising	1,500	
Sales promotion	250	
		1,750
Gross contribution	16,050	
Units sold	10,000	
Gross contribution per unit		1,605

Figure 10.5 Contribution Per Unit Report

product—costs that do not disappear if the product disappears. There are, of course, arguments about whether the costs disappear or not. Some of the direct costs that are allocated do not go away completely, but they can be cut without too much difficulty.

The reason for preparing the report like this is that the profit responsibilities of the marketing manager are clearly identified; there is no confusion caused by the allocation of overhead (period costs as they are sometimes called), the misuse of transfer prices, and putting expenses into classifications such as wages, office expenses, raw materials, etc. (To avoid the confusion often caused by using artificial transfer prices, it is necessary to leave out the cost of goods sold and work simply on local contribution. This would apply where components were brought in from another factory or another country at an artificially low or high price. Such a price, if not left out of the report, would distort the picture of the results, making it difficult to draw conclusions.)

Primary Ratios of Turnover and Profit

Since profitability is one of the primary aims of business, and one of the best measures of efficiency, it is important to establish the relationship between profits and investment in the business. Increased sales volume is at best a short-term indication of successful growth. Real growth comes from the ability of management successfully to employ additional capital at a satisfactory rate of return. The return on investment ROI formula was developed by E.I. DuPont de Nemours & Company and popularized by General Motors in an effort to arrive at an effective, valid measurement of the return achieved on an investment, no matter what type of disparate businesses might be compared. The method of calculating ROI is shown in Figure 10.6. This formula can be used for a number of purposes, e.g.:

- Comparison of one year's results with another.
- Noting a trend over five years.
- Comparing one division of a company with another.
- Setting targets for each unit or subsidiary.
- Identifying the influence of building blocks.

It is at the end that the formula can perhaps best be used by marketing managers.

As can be seen from Figure 10.6 the ROI can be divided into percentage profit on sales (return on sales) and the rate of asset turnover (sales divided by total assets or capital employed), which means that a low return on capital employed can be due to falling profit margins, low rate of asset turnover, or both. A good illustration of the formula can be

Figure 10.6 ROI Formula

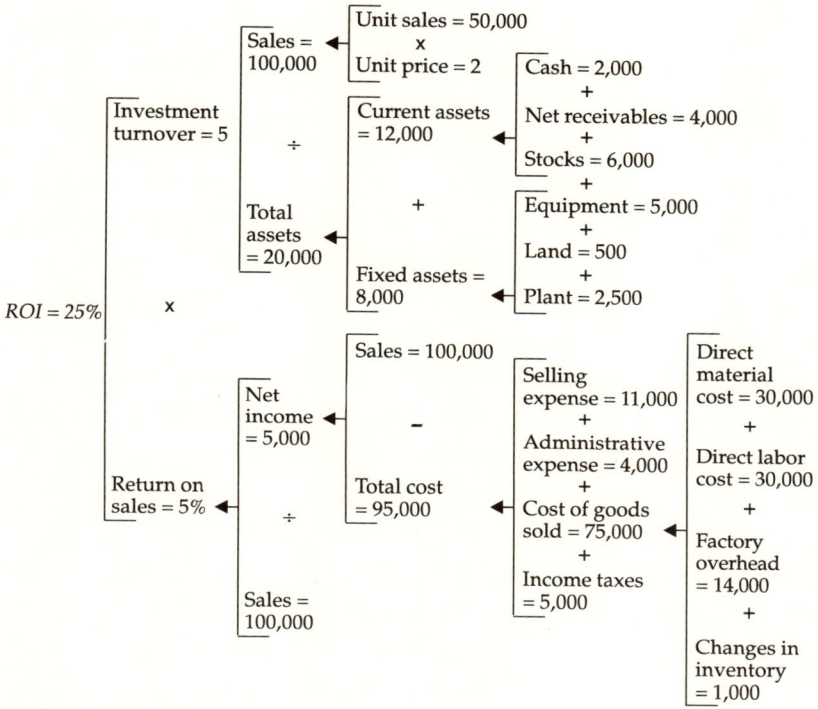

```
ROI = 25% = Investment turnover (5) × Return on sales (5%)

Investment turnover = 5 = Sales (100,000) ÷ Total assets (20,000)
  Sales = 100,000 = Unit sales (50,000) × Unit price (2)
  Total assets = 20,000 = Current assets (12,000) + Fixed assets (8,000)
    Current assets = 12,000 = Cash (2,000) + Net receivables (4,000) + Stocks (6,000)
    Fixed assets = 8,000 = Equipment (5,000) + Land (500) + Plant (2,500)

Return on sales = 5% = Net income (5,000) ÷ Sales (100,000)
  Net income = 5,000 = Sales (100,000) − Total cost (95,000)
  Total cost = 95,000 = Selling expense (11,000) + Administrative expense (4,000) + Cost of goods sold (75,000) + Income taxes (5,000)
  Cost of goods sold = 75,000 = Direct material cost (30,000) + Direct labor cost (30,000) + Factory overhead (14,000) + Changes in inventory (1,000)
```

Read from right to left.

seen in the comparison between a department store and a supermarket, each of which had an ROI of 20 percent. The supermarket achieved this by a turnover of assets of ten times per year and a profit margin of 2 percent. The department store had an asset turnover of two times per year and a profit margin of 10 percent.

ROI Per Product

Apart from external comparisons or those for the separate divisions or units within the company, calculations can be made of the return on assets managed (ROAM) for each product group. This assumes that, at the budgeting stage, the different building blocks can be fairly apportioned without too much difficulty (see Figure 10.7). In this case a forecast has been made of the ROI for each product group. Fixed costs at their written-down value (see Figure 10.1) have been allocated to product groups A, B and C. Costs of service departments X and Y are allocated (on the basis of hours worked, perhaps) to the three product groups.

A sales forecast is made and the variable, fixed, and apportioned costs are subtracted to arrive at a trading profit. This gives a forecast ROI for each product group—C is a clear winner!

Before taking action, however, and dropping product group B, it is necessary to look at what would happen to the capital assets currently employed in producing B—would they, in fact, be released? Are all the direct costs associated with producing B actually dispensable? Is there a better use for the fixed assets?

Other Ratios

Besides ROI there are a number of other ratios that are important to the marketing manager, e.g., profit margins on sales

$$\frac{\text{net profit after taxes}}{\text{sales}} : \frac{\$90,000}{\$13,000,000} = 3\%$$

and activity ratios such as

- Ratio of receivables (debtors) to sales.
- Average collection period.

$$\frac{\text{accounts receivable} \times 360}{\text{annual sales}}$$

Assets Employed						
			Product Groups		Service Departments	
	Total	A	B	C	X	Y
Fixed Assets						
Assumed current cost	210,000	120,000	20,000	50,000	15,000	5,000
Less accumulated depreciation	140,000	90,000	5,000	39,000	5,000	1,000
Written-Down Value	70,000	30,000	15,000	11,000	10,000	4,000
Net Current Assets						
Stocks	30,000	10,000	6,000	3,000	8,000	3,000
Trade debtors	40,000	25,000	10,000	5,000	—	—
Less trade creditors	(20,000)	(9,000)	(4,000)	(2,000)	(3,000)	(2,000)
	50,000	26,000	12,000	6,000	5,000	1,000
Net Trading Assets Employed	120,000	56,000	27,000	17,000	15,000	5,000
Apportionment of service departments	—	11,000	6,000	3,000	(15,000)	(5,000)
Net Trading Assets Employed in Product Groups	120,000	67,000	33,000	20,000		

Sales Forecast				
		Product Groups		
	Total	A	B	C
Sales	173,000	100,000	33,000	40,000
Less variable cost of sales	140,000	82,900	25,200	30,900
Total Contribution	33,000	16,100	7,800	9,100
Less separable fixed costs	10,000	4,000	3,500	2,500
Direct Product Profit	23,000	12,100	14,300	6,600
Less apportioned common fixed costs	5,000	1,900	1,800	1,300
Trading Profit	18,000	10,200	2,500	5,300
Forecast ROI	15%	15.2%	7.6%	25.5%

Figure 10.7   A Manufacturing Company—ROI Forecast to December 31

stock (inventory) turnover

$$\frac{\text{total stock}}{\text{annual sales}}$$

Such ratios can assist in deciding where profitability or cash flow can be improved.

Costing and Pricing

There are times when the marketing manager is confronted with the need to relate prices to costs, so that general management can start to consider resource allocation. (Naturally the final deciding factor is what the market will bear, since if the price is wrong for the market there is little point in arguing about its relation to costs.)

The most common method of arriving at a price for a manufactured product is by absorption costing. The accountant calculates the cost of producing one unit of each product at the normal capacity level of the existing plant, adds a satisfactory profit margin, and arrives at the price. The problem with this, as seen by the marketing manager, is the basis of the absorption of overhead. While it is obvious that, at the end of the day, all overhead costs must be covered, the methods used to estimate the rate of absorption in advance are always open to question (because they are a matter of judgment). In his book *An Insight into Management Accounting,* Professor John Sizer presents this in Figure 10.8.

It shows the price that, at a given level of capacity, will give each product a certain profit margin. The danger with using this method, except as a guide or starting point, is that business may be lost if the plant is not working at full capacity and orders are rejected because they are not offered at full price. Equally, however, being unaware of the amount of overheads that must be absorbed and charging

	Production $	Fixed Costs Selling and Distribution $	Administration $
Annual fixed cost	30,000	5,000	2,000
Basis of absorption	Direct labor hours 60,000	Cost of production 100,000	Cost of production 100,000
Absorption rate	$0.50 per direct labor hour	5% of cost production	2% of cost production

Suggested Selling Prices

	Product A $	Product B $	Product C $
Direct labor	4 (10 h)	2 (5 h)	8 (20 h)
Direct material	5	4	5
Direct expense	1	—	2
Prime Cost	10	6	15
Production overhead			
Variable	5	1.5	5
Fixed	5	2.50	10
Cost of Production	20	10	30
Selling and distribution costs:			
Variable	1.50	0.25	0.75
Fixed	1	0.50	1.50
Administration overhead			
Fixed	0.40	0.20	0.60
Total Cost	22.90	10.95	32.85
Profit Margin	2.29 (10%)	1.64 (15%)	6.57 (20%)
Selling Price	25.19	12.59	39.42
Marginal Cost	16.50	7.75	20.75

Figure 10.8 Determination of Selling Prices by Absorption Costing

low prices can also lead to disaster. (The airlines, with a very high proportion of overhead costs in their total cost, are always being tempted to offer prices that offer a profit on the marginal/direct cost, to fill the airplane. The reckoning comes when the overheads—interest payments, staff costs, and maintenance—are not covered within the accounting period.)

A development of absorption costing as a basis for pricing is the use of the rate of return. This starts from the ROI concepts shown earlier. In a multidivision company the board may well establish that the ROI target is to be 15 percent. This must have its effect not only on all the building blocks, as shown in Chapter 11, but also on profitability—which is reflected in the price to be charged. To arrive at the percentage markup required, start the ROI formula in Figure 10.6 with the planned (or desired) rate of return and read from left to right. Suppose this is 25 percent, as shown. Then

$$\% \text{ markup on cost} = \frac{\text{capital employed}}{\text{total cost}} \times \text{Desired rate of return}$$

$$\text{e.g.} \quad \frac{20,000}{95,000} \times 25\% = 5.263\%$$

This approach again assumes static capacity and cost figures.

The only way to avoid this is to use marginal (direct cost) pricing (see Figure 10.8), i.e., look at the question of what would happen to *total* profits if prices of particular products were raised or lowered. Since pricing decisions (having assessed the market's level of acceptance) involve planning for the future, they should deal solely with estimated future revenues, expenses, and outlays of capital. Past outlays that give rise to fixed costs are historical and unchangeable. Short-term decisions should consider what can be changed, or will change. Sunk costs are sunk and should bear very little on plans for the future.

Budgets

A budget is a quantitative expression of a plan of action and an aid to coordination and implementation. Budgets can be formulated for the organization as a whole or for any subunit. The budget summarizes objectives and quantifies the expectations regarding future income, cash flows, financial status, and supporting plans.

The central function of budgeting in the management process can be derived from the chart shown in Figure 10.9,

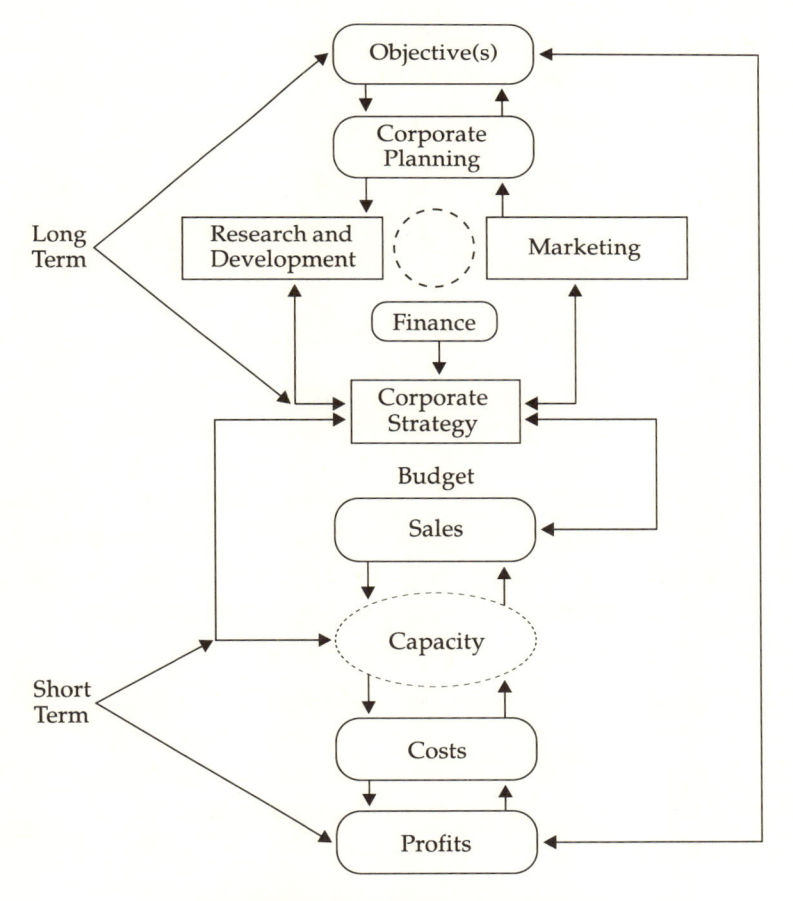

Figure 10.9 Management Process

which illustrates in monetary terms the standard targets that are expected from revenue and costs. For example, the marketing manager's sales forecast and marketing plan will be translated into a budget that will cover

- Orders expected (by product or by sales territory, etc.).
- Deliveries (by quantity and value).
- Marketing expenses such as
  - advertising
  - sales promotion
  - sales staff
  - sales office
  - product management
  - market research

The purpose of budgeting is to enable managers to compare actual results with budgeted results and identify the causes of the variances that are thus exposed, as shown in the following chart.

There are two items to be considered here:

- The importance of the "variance" rather than the accuracy of the budget.

- The need to examine the variances in terms of their relative importance—a variance of 25 percent is much more important than a variance of 5 percent—even though the quantities demonstrate the opposite.

Table 10.1 Monthly Budget/Variance Report

Month	Item	Budget	Actual	Variance	Percentage (V of B)
December	Orders	10,000	9,500	500	−5%
	Deliveries	8,000	7,000	1,000	−12½%
	Expenses	1,000	1,250	250	+25%

To put the question of budgeting in context, the marketing budget would be only one of a series of revenue and capital budgets that must be produced annually to provide a framework (and a forward look) for the directors of the business. In addition, in the process of producing budgets, two systems of analysis may well be in place (or under consideration) in some businesses: Zero-base budgeting and overhead value analysis.

Zero-base budgeting starts from the principle that a budget for the year should not simply take last year's situation and carry it forward into the next period. The opportunity should be seized to examine the whole pattern of expenditure, and to evaluate the underlying need for each item. If carried to extremes, the process of starting from scratch each year is very time-consuming. It is, however, worthwhile to apply the principle to sections of the business each year.

Overhead value analysis questions the assumptions behind the existence of all staff departments, by asking each line department: "As a customer of the personnel department (for example), what benefits do you receive?"—then matching the answer against the view of the personnel department of what benefits it provides. This questions the foundations of the fixed cost aspects of the budget.

11
DECISION MAKING AND ACCOUNTING

Marketing actions cause financial impact on the company. At the same time, marketing managers should be able to use financial and accounting information to make better decisions. In this chapter a number of decision-making tools are examined and their functions described.

Cash-Flow Analysis and Measurement

Much of the result, favorable or unfavorable, of marketing action is demonstrated in cash flow. Although closely connected, cash flow and profit are not the same. Profit is defined in accounting terms as "a concept designed to measure the overall performance of the company," and it is open to various measurement techniques and accounting conventions. Cash flow is not a measure of the company's performance, and it is not subject to conventions. Either the company has cash or it has not.

A lack of cash is critical. A company can sustain losses for a time without suffering permanent damage, but a company that has no cash is insolvent and in imminent danger of bankruptcy, no matter what its profit picture may be. Thus planning the flow of cash is vital to the continuity of the business.

In the longer term, the idea of cash flow is of vital importance to the appraisal of capital investment. It can be seen that the real cost to the business of a new project that requires investment is the actual net amount of cash that flows *out* of the business as a result of the investment decision; the return to the business on that project is the actual amount of cash that flows *into* the business from the project during its lifetime.

Marketing managers need to be able to assess cash-flow calculations made by other departments for the current forecast in businesses that are seasonally sensitive, in businesses where large contracts are signed at irregular intervals, for investment in new projects, or for significant marketing expenditures (such as an advertising campaign). Cash-flow forecasting can be prepared as a summary of the transactions expected to be recorded in the cash account of the business during the forecast period (see Figure 11.1). This is especially desirable in a situation like the one shown in Figure 11.2 where seasonal effects are so marked that a bank loan is needed at a certain stage during the year.

Project Evaluation

For investing in particular projects (such as the development of new products) it is also important to forecast the flow of cash (both negative and positive) so as to argue whether the project is, of itself, a good use of the company's money. Three aspects need to be looked at: capital employed in existing product groups, capital invested in new products, and how such investment can be evaluated. The capital employed in a business can be divided into

1. Fixed assets.
2. Working capital. (Also called circulating capital, it is equal to current assets [stocks, cash, and easily negotiable securities, and receivables] *less* current liabilities [payables, dividends, etc.]).

	Dollars
Receipts	
Debtors outstanding	850
Past month's credit sales	420
This month's cash sales	290
Other receipts	—
Total Receipts	1,560
Payments	
Trade creditors outstanding	300
Purchases	65
Wages	350
Salaries	150
Promotion expenses	45
Rent and rates	200
Other expenses (detailed)	75
Capital expenditure	30
Dividends and interest	25
Taxation (VAT, etc.)	40
Total Payments	1,280
Net Receipts (or Payments)	280
Cash balance (or overdraft) at beginning of month	Z
Cash balance (or overdraft) at end of month	287

Figure 11.1 Cash-Flow Forecast

The dynamic aspects of cash are shown in Figure 11.3, which also shows the relationship between fixed and working capital. This demonstrates that in the trading cycle, cash flows via payables into raw materials, work in progress, and finished products, and then into receivables. Profit created by trading comes into the cash pool via receivables. Fixed assets and longer-term liabilities are difficult to alter quickly or in the short term. However, it is possible to affect the cash situation by manipulating the variables.

194 / Management Skills in Marketing

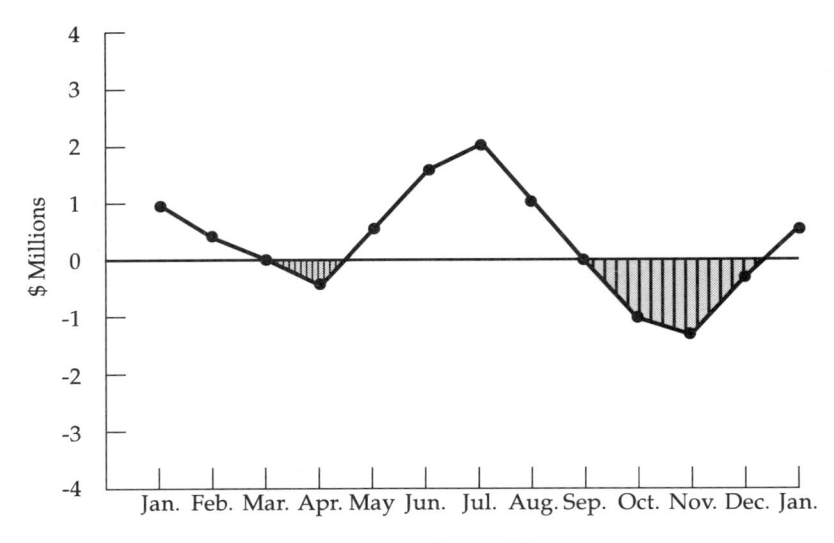

Figure 11.2 Net Cash Position Forecast

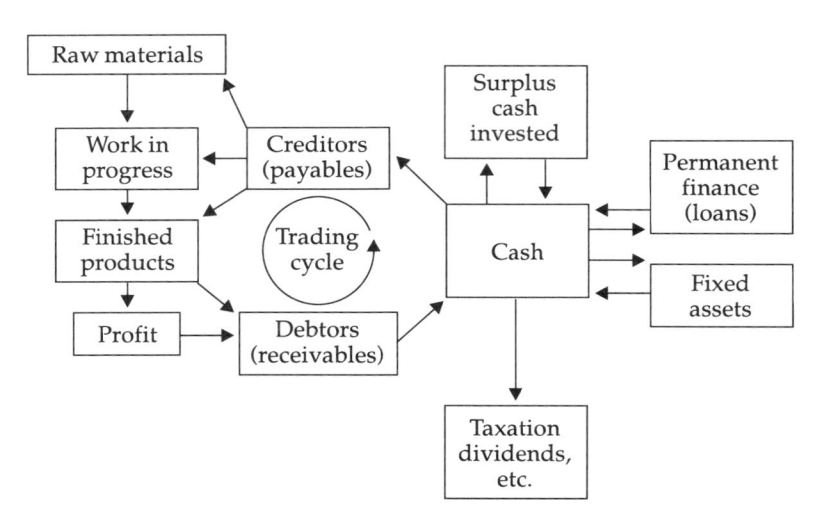

Figure 11.3 Trading Cycle

Influence on Cash Flow

Market managers can and often are expected to have some influence on cash flow. Marketing efforts with an existing product can mean increased coverage of the market; to cope with this there would need to be increased cash tied up in receivables, as well as in finished products in order to cover increased expectations. A shortage of cash can imply action in the form of quicker collection of receivables, running down stocks and reducing work in progress. Accounts departments will usually help by extending credit taken from suppliers; production departments can help by reducing the length of the production cycle.

There is usually a trade-off. Extending credit taken from suppliers can result in prompt payment discounts being lost. Running down stocks can cause sales to be lost, pressure on debtors can cause loss of goodwill. Such penalties must be set off against their positive influence on cash flow.

This decision process can be taken further and applied to the ROI pattern shown in Chapter 10. For example, although the launch of a new product will involve manufacturing, selling, and administrative costs, and the profit margin will need to cover these in order to produce a satisfactory percentage on that arm of the ROI chart, the same product launch will increase working capital by increasing stocks of all kinds, probably an increase of net receivables (minus payables), and possibly will have involved increasing fixed assets in the form of new machinery. The turnover rate will be influenced by the latter if the targeted ROI figure is to be reached.

Capital Investment in New Products

The detailed scheduling of investment in new products (or projects) and the return on that investment is usually left to those who like working with figures. The more creative marketing people believe they are above such things. Even when the approach is explained there are still those who find the matter either too difficult or irrelevant to the real business. The intention here is to show some of the signposts along the way.

For small businesses, the product may well be the future of the business itself, so profit and loss calculations are a vitally important part of the Business Plan. A business that starts with a good idea needs to look ahead to the point where the investment (bank loan, share offer, mortgage, whatever) begins to pay off. Thus calculations apply not only to products, but to the entire business.

For some services (such as consultancy), there may be less need to consider the payback possibilities of an investment. However, for capital-intensive services (such as the purchase of a hotel or an aircraft) careful analysis is critical as shown in Table 11.1.

It is valuable first to create the forecasts of different aspects of the project, and then examine the assumptions behind those forecasts. First, forecasts must be made of capacity and production required, stocks and sales turnover in units, to see whether the project will actually work. Such forecasts can either be shown on an annual scale, or

Table 11.1 Net Cash Inflow

Year	1	2	3	4	5	Total
Item	$000s					
Investment in plant, etc.	(60)	(30)	—	(10)	—	(100)
Profit after tax	—	(10)	5	35	50	80
Depreciation	—	6	9	7	4	26
Working capital	—	(15)	(6)	(3)	24	—
Net cash inflow	–60	–49	8	29	78	+6

( ) = minus

detailed as a series of action stages on a new product launch, for example

- Idea search.
- Screening.
- Test marketing.
- Launch and primary diffusion.
- Total coverage/saturation.
- Decline.

The planning horizon has a great deal to do with the product's expected life cycle.

Second, make forecasts of investment required, along with the necessary assumptions, split into buildings, machinery, etc., and the annual requirements over the length of the project's life. Third, make similarly charted forecasts of revenue, together with assumptions of price levels. Fourth, make a kind of profit and loss statement forecast for each year of the planned project's life. From these forecasts an assumption about working capital requirements over the period must be charted.

Evaluating Investment

The principal methods of making decisions as to whether an investment is worthwhile are

- Payback period.
- Profit on sales.
- Return on investment.
- Discounted cash flow or present value. (See Table 11.2.)

Of these, return on investment (See Chapter 10) appears to be more concerned with target setting and analysis than

Table 11.2 Present Value Calculations

	−60	−49	8	29	78	Result
12% PV factor	x 0.893 = −54	x 0.797 = −39	x 0.712 = 6	x 0.635 = 18	x 0.567 = 44	−25
5% PV factor	x 0.952 = −57	x 0.907 = −44	x 0.864 = 7	x 0.823 = 24	x 0.783 = 61	−9
2% PV factor	x 0.980 = −59	x 0.961 = −47	x 0.942 = 8	x 0.924 = 27	x 0.906 = 71	0

with future projects (though it provides a basis for discounted cash flow calculations); profit on sales or return on sales ratio is a good measure for annual observation but, because the level of investment is often disregarded, it is difficult to use for new projects.

The payback method works on the basis of the number of years it will take for a project to pay for itself out of its earnings (a method, in domestic life, used in discussion of the cost of insulation against the reduction in heating bills). By this method, the project that will pay for itself in the shortest time after the date of the original investment is the winner (see Table 11.3).

Based on the payback method, Project A would be preferred because its payback period is two years, whereas Project B's payback period is three years. Some of the disadvantages of the system are evident here—the ROI for Project B is in fact higher; no account is taken of profits arising after the investment has been paid for; definition of profits is not clear; and the time value of money is ignored.

Table 11.3 Payback Calculation

	Project A	Project B
Cost	$10,000	$10,000
Estimated Future Profits		
Year 1	5,000	2,000
Year 2	5,000	4,000
Year 3	2,000	4,000
Year 4	2,000	6,000

The present value method (or discounted cash flow) has as its base the calculation of the present value of future sums of money:

$100 invested at 10 percent per annum (compound) would accumulate to $1,000.

$1,000 received in two years' time has a present value of $100. Present value is thus the reverse of compound interest.

One can therefore use the following formula:

$$P = S \times \frac{1}{(1 + r)^n}$$

where

P = present value

S = future sum

r = interest rate expressed as a ratio (10% = 0.1)

n = number of years

The yardstick against which a project is judged is whether the present value of cash inflows exceeds the cost of the project, when using a reasonable rate of interest, such as the alternative opportunity for investing the capital (in building societies, or gilt-edged securities). For example, to arrive at net cash inflow, the items shown in Table 11.1 need to be considered over a period of perhaps five years.

(Profits have been taken realistically as profits after tax. Depreciation is added back as part of the net cash inflow. Working capital includes stocks, cash, and net receivables.) Apply a present value factor as shown in the formula to each of the net cash inflow figures. The result is shown in Table 11.3.

This demonstrates that the rate of return on the project is 2 percent. Doing this kind of exercise allows some further work to be done to discover what changes need to be made in the initial forecast to bring the project up to a reasonable or acceptable rate of return. (Note: A table of present values is a useful tool for speeding the calculation.)

Opportunity Cost

Other problems arise when it is necessary to decide between a number of conflicting claims for limited funds—particularly when the results, good or bad, can vary not only in the view of the forecaster but also because of external conditions. In her book *Financial Tools for Marketing Administration*, Letricia Gayle Rayburn discusses what she calls "quantified regrets" to demonstrate the cost of the best foregone conclusion. The idea is useful when making short-term decisions. Suppose a company wishes to invest $100,000 in marketing in a way that will produce the best result. There are four possible alternatives as set out in Table 11.4.

As can be seen, the forecast return from each of the alternatives used for the investment depends upon external conditions, but not one is clearly the winner in all

Table 11.4 Alternative Investment Results

Alternatives	External Conditions		
	Excellent	Average	Poor
Advertising Product A	+10,000	+6,000	–4,000
Putting A into a new market	+30,000	+10,000	–1,000
Relaunching Product B	+12,000	+7,500	–3,000
Producing Product C	+8,000	+8,000	—

circumstances. Look at the best possible return in each external condition and then subtract from it the return for a particular alternative. The result is a Quantified Regret Table (Table 11.5).

Putting A into a new market now shows the lowest quantified regret figure under all conditions. This approach could become more sophisticated by attaching probabilities to the external conditions and multiplying the payoff by the probability (e.g., 50% likelihood = 0.5 x).

Table 11.5 Quantified Regret Table

Alternatives	External Conditions		
	Excellent	Average	Poor
Advertising Product A	20,000	4,000	4,000
Putting A into a new market	—	—	1,000
Relaunching Product B	18,000	2,500	3,000
Producing Product C	22,000	2,000	—

Break-Even Charts, Profit-Volume Relationships, and Limiting Factors

In the discussions between the marketing manager and the production manager there is often a need to understand the relationships between costs (of various types), volumes of output, and profit. Following John Sizer's example, it is probable that a break-even chart showing an area is more likely to represent the truth than one that simply shows one point. The basis is still the fixed cost of the production of units of output, shown as a straight line (see Figure 11.4). Since variable cost must be directly related to each unit of output the line is straight, sales also are shown as a regular line rising from zero to and beyond the point where the sales line crosses the total cost line (the break-even point). Although for many purposes this is an easily understood demonstration of the relationship between costs, output and profit, it encompasses a number of assumptions.

1. It takes no account of stock changes, and assumes that sales and output are equal.
2. It relates to one product or a constant mix (in volume terms) of products.
3. It makes no allowance for variations in the cost picture with changes in output (fixed costs becoming semivariable, for example), or for variations in the selling price per unit.
4. It assumes that volume changes are the only ones to affect costs and that inaccuracies in the calculation are shown up only in profit variances.

The profit-volume chart (Figure 11.5) demonstrates the percentage of total capacity (on the horizontal axis) which, with given fixed costs, is related to a particular contribution level. Starting at the bottom left, the loss is the equivalent of the fixed costs of manufacture. Proceed to the right along

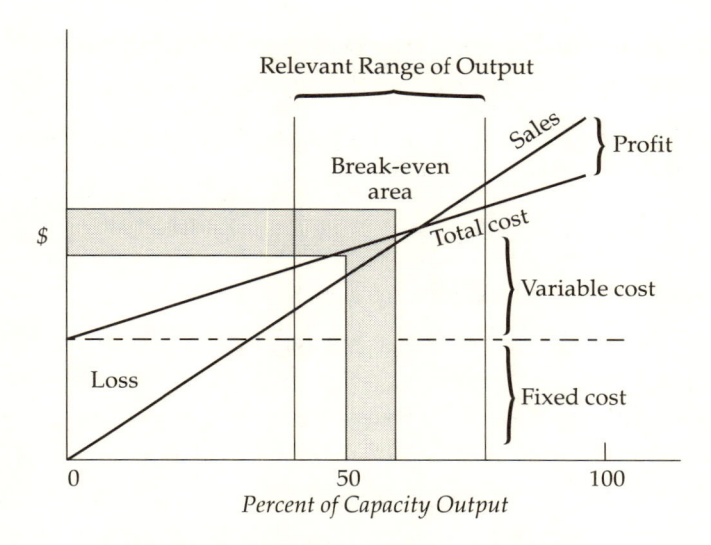

Figure 11.4 Break-Even Area Chart

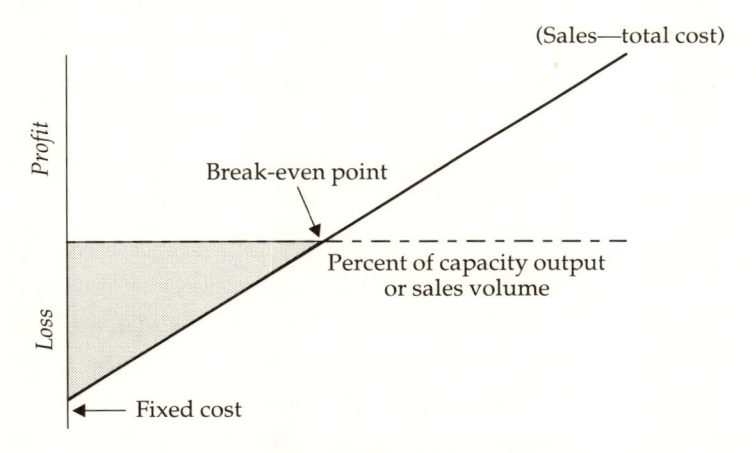

Figure 11.5 Profit-Volume Chart

the horizontal axis of sales volume where the line of contribution rises to meet the horizontal; and a break-even point is reached when the contribution is equal to the amount of fixed costs. Plotting it on a graph as in Figure

11.5 is easier to understand than working with a formula, but for those who prefer it the formula is

$$\text{break-even volume} = \frac{\text{total fixed cost}}{1 - \left\{\dfrac{\text{total variable cost}}{\text{total sales}}\right\}}$$

Contribution and Fixed Expenditure

Generally speaking, a business with high fixed costs, such as a paper-making company or an airline (or even, under certain circumstances, a firm of management consultants) will have a high break-even point, but the contribution rate is usually higher because of the low level of variable direct costs. In such companies, the strategy is to maximize turnover and, as a result, spend large amounts of money on promotion activities designed to get the extra turnover. In a business with low contribution (defined as the difference between revenue and direct costs) the main emphasis is likely to be on increasing the contribution by efficient operation—efficient use of the direct costs. (Typically in a supermarket, resulting in careful purchasing, better use of floor displays, better staff utilization, etc.)

Limiting Factors

For the purpose of explanation it is usually assumed that the company has one product or a standard mix of products. In real life, there are never enough resources to do everything, and a choice has to be made. The profitability of the product mix is affected by one or more limiting factors in companies, for example:

- The type of raw materials
- An item of the plant
- Skilled labor

- Floor space
- Cash

Therefore, the limiting factors need to be clearly identified. There may be a whole range of factors, in which case a certain amount of linear programming might be needed to solve the problem. In general, the rule is that the order of preference in which products should be sold or manufactured can be decided by calculating the contribution each product makes to the limiting factor. For example, if the limiting factor is plant hours, then the product's usage of plant hours divided into contribution per unit gives a contribution rate per plant hour. Each product can then be ranked in order of its contribution per plant hour.

If, however, the problem is underutilization of capacity, then additional profits are computed by multiplying additional sales by the contribution per product. Later, deduct from such additional profit any increase in fixed costs that resulted from the acceptance of an order. Direct costs—those costs that arise because of the production of a product, and that are likely to disappear when it is discontinued—should be used as the basis of assessing where resources are best put, because they allow marketing managers to think about contribution unencumbered by worries about overheads and fixed (period) costs.

12
CONTROLLING MARKETING EFFECTIVENESS

About twelve years ago a colleague of mine, Andrew Symington, who was involved in running courses in marketing, began to concern himself with a very real, down-to-earth problem. How does the marketing man argue with the managing director (or the other members of the management team) that his allocation of funds is effective? Managing directors then, as now, were concerned that while efforts to improve manufacturing productivity could be seen to yield results (or not!) the costs of marketing seemed to be largely a matter of faith or hope. Then, as now, the costs of marketing were increasing rapidly, and this fact was creating a demand for more effective means of measuring the contribution that marketing activities made to company profit.

While sophisticated forms of assessment and control are normal in both manufacturing and administration, measurement of the contribution made by marketing activities to profitability is often haphazard and incomplete. So how is the managing director to be satisfied? Is it enough for the finance director of a company to attend a marketing course to discover if the $1 million advertising budget is really contributing to profit?

Limitations on Control Activities

Currently there are a number of limitations to control marketing expenditures. Even today marketing consultants can urge managers to apply ruthless and consistent pressure on specific areas of expenditure in order to assess effectiveness, which is really another form of a marketing productivity audit. The problem with this kind of examination is that it is usually limited to asking if activities have been performed according to plan. As a result of such control efforts there may be an evident need for better market research, more creative advertising, or more effort in getting to a specific group of customers—increased coverage of a particular segment. This is probably all that is realistic once resources have been committed, the sales force has been disposed and the advertising agency has been briefed. It is too late to reconsider the allocation of expenditure.

Improving Allocation

The control function should not be limited to checking on whether the resources that are planned have, in fact, been used. The purpose is to try to improve the quality of the allocation process, to optimize the advertising budget, to decide whether money is better spent on more market research or on labor-saving machinery in the warehouse and to ensure that the sales effort is used to its maximum effect (the maximum profit, if this can be factually assessed).

To start, it is worth examining the breakeven chart, (see Figure 11.4) to see what the likely effects can be of changing some of the parameters. If fixed costs are reduced, then clearly more profit will result—but fixed costs (in the form of stocks, for example) may have an important bearing on the likelihood of sales reaching beyond the new break-even point. And what about price concessions—will they make it easier to increase the market share or will they simply postpone the break-even point without any resulting increase in profit? It requires time and concentration to examine, during the planning process, the different options available.

Looking only at the short-term problems means the possibility that there could be concentration on problems rather than opportunities; so much effort will be spent (both time and money) on solving problems that there will be none left for opportunities. And for the marketing manager to succeed in today's environment, he has to know how to take advantage of opportunities.

Controllable Factors

The marketing manager is surrounded with so many noncontrollable factors (see Figure 3.5) that to find a few over which he can exercise some power and influence is a great relief. Of course the major noncontrollable factor is the customer—which is why it is so difficult to allocate responsibility and results to any particular factor or factors. A satisfactory marketing result is usually the outcome of the correct marketing mix applied at *that* moment, in *that* place, to *that* customer.

The factors that are controllable are usually listed as the four Ps of marketing— Product, Price, Promotion, and Place. But there is much more to each factor than a simple mnemonic would suggest (see Chapter 4).

Product and Price

The *product* is not only the physical, tangible item produced in the factory, but also its attributes in the eyes of the customer: its level of quality, its level of technology, and the design and packaging that surround it. In a service business, the intangibility factor is extended. For the client or customer, it covers the whole experience from first contact to final satisfaction. The physical production of the service is aimed at the logistics of providing what has been promised; customer satisfaction also depends on the treatment received in the service experience.

The *price*, which looms so large in the minds of salesmen, and often gives misleading signals to producers and consumers, includes not only the absolute level of price, i.e., in relation to all other uses for personal resources (cash), but also the influence on price of how large the product looms in the total cost of production. In the construction of a television set, the TV tube makes up some 25 to 30 percent of the cost of components. To produce one resistor for the set at 15 cents, the proportion of the total cost is insignificant, and therefore the price level and the view of it by the buyer is hardly affected. (It may well be influenced by competition, or total expenditure over a year, however.) Price influence on buying patterns might also include the ability or willingness of the producer to provide credit or to give discounts for large quantities. Groups of companies who have central buying offices—particularly in the retail trade, and in fast moving consumer goods—*expect* quantity discounts. It may, indeed, be the primary reason for the existence of the group.

Promotion and Place

Promotion is also not simple. As a controllable buying factor, different aspects may influence purchasers (and potential purchasers). Straightforward media advertising is one aspect to be considered; so is the company's image and reputation, which might be supported by specific public relations activities or policies. Sales promotion other than advertising can be considered separately, involving special help to agents or distributors, attendance at exhibitions, training of retail staff, show-cards, giveaways, and gimmicks (the list is almost endless, but will vary depending on the type of company concerned). Direct mail has, in the 1990s, become an even more intensely used form of promotion; more accurate market identification and the use of focused databases has seen to it. It must be one of every business's controllable factors. Promotion will also include the deployment, effectiveness, and relationships of salesmen, which would include all those who have contact with customers and are involved in persuading customers to purchase.

The *Place* factor is also controllable, and its effect on potential purchasers must be established. It includes product availability, the convenience of a distribution channel ("You can buy this in any supermarket or corner shop") or that the supply is assured when the assembly line requires it; it includes the reliability of delivery, the level of stocks, and the quality of the service provided in ensuring easy installation of the product. For service businesses, the place factor includes convenience of a local office (lawyer, travel agent), reachability of departure and destination points (buses, trains, airlines), and availability of appropriate specialists (consulting engineers, insurance company agents).

The objective in controlling the effectiveness of these factors is to balance the different parts of each factor (which is assessable in money terms) against each other, which will give (or has given) better results.

- An improved range of products *or* more salesmen.
- Developing a new market *or* more effort and expenditure on research and development.

- More effort in national advertising against better packaging to help distributors.
- Reduced prices or better credit terms.

Allocating Funds

Chapter 4 discussed the use of factor analysis in order to establish the emphasis on factors that would have a clinching effect on selected market segments. At this stage the marketing manager is concerned with checking what has happened, so that improvements can be made in the allocation of funds in the future. He therefore needs to look carefully at the funds that have been provided for each factor, what the objective might be specifically for that factor, and how far the result (or output) has justified the level of input.

A problem can arise in this analytical approach in the allocation of staff activities and their costs. Staff activities would include such nonproductive services as market research and marketing planning. Here again they should be examined and allocated to result-producing activities.

There is a school of consultancy that advocates analysis of overhead activity by drawing up two lists of customer requirements: one list is created by the operator of the service, such as market research, showing the quantity, quality, and cost of the service that his customers require; the other is created by the customers—product managers, sales managers, advertising managers, perhaps—showing the requirement they have, in terms of quantity, quality, and price, for the service being discussed. In so far as these lists may be quantified, it would appear to be a valuable basis for deciding on the scope and cost of services and other overheads.

Inherent Product Appeal

To control marketing effectiveness it is important to examine the relationship among the different factors, and in particular to try to assess inherent product appeal. Not all sales, in fact, are the result of selling (see Figure 2.1). A large proportion of the revenue of many companies is customers seeking out a particular product, not as a result of selling effort. This thought leads to two further points of discussion. If there are two products or product lines that have roughly the same revenue, and selling and sales promotion activity is withdrawn from both, it is extremely unlikely that sales will drop to zero, even over a long period. Not only that but the amount (or proportion) of revenue lost will also vary, which will demonstrate the differing effect of the input of promotion activities on different product lines.

If, then, similar amounts of money, time, and effort spent on selling and sales promotion produce differing results in terms of product line revenue, there must be a point where effort should be shifted to *improving* the product rather than *promoting* it. This point will vary from one industry or business to another, but there must come a point in each product's existence when it can be said: "When more than 'x' percent of the selling price is absorbed by persuasion costs, then something should be done to modify, or improve or scrap the product."

Equally the reverse of this situation also demands an unbiased examination. If the product sells itself, what need is there for a sales force or other selling activity? This particular point often arises in service industries, where this problem is particularly acute. For the most part the service industries—including professional service providers such as architects and tradesmen such as plumbers—

are saying: "If you have need of this service, choose us." But this is hardly a dynamic selling approach, if it is selling at all. It is pointless for the plumber who has some spare time in the summer to go door to door asking if there are any broken pipes to be repaired. Yet he wants to be the plumber who is selected when a plumbing disaster happens. Thus it can (and should) be argued that if the persuasion costs are *less* than "y" percent of selling price, then serious consideration should be given to scrapping the selling apparatus and finding some other way to bring the product to the attention of buyers. Many companies complain endlessly about the increasing cost of salesmen, travel, commissions, training, etc., but are not sufficiently radical to examine the alternatives, such as telephone selling, direct marketing (taking out ads in magazines) and direct mail, because this demands challenging the conventional wisdom about what a salesman achieves!

Marketing Cost Analysis

In spite of considerable progress made in recent years (much of it attributable to the popular Finance for Nonfinancial Executives training courses) there are still many companies that lump together all costs incurred after production as overheads. This overhead is then allocated or apportioned in an arbitrary and unconsidered way to different products, sales regions, or markets. The problem seems to be two-fold: deciding whether it is of value to allocate costs to territories, customers, and products in light of the difficulty of modifying existing information collection and distribution systems; and the actual allocation and apportioning of costs.

Present systems of collecting and analyzing costs are usually based on natural expense classifications: wages and salaries, invoicing, transport, or advertising. Thus the marketing manager can be attacked on the fact that costs are rising, but he has no way of establishing what has caused the rise in costs or where those costs apply. The argument is, therefore, not difficult to sustain that the information system should enable (help) the marketing manager to examine the cost structure per territory, product, and customer. Territories would be chosen on the basis that total revenue from a territory is related to the cost of servicing it. Products would be classified by the differences in sales volume and value. Customers could be classified in groups according to the annual value of business received (see Figure 3.7).

To arrive at the contribution per territory, customer group, or product line, it is first necessary to identify the costs that would be saved if the company stopped selling in a particular territory, or supplying a group of customers, or offering certain products. The basis of allocation is shown in Table 12.1.

Establishing and Checking on Objectives

Because this method of analyzing the costs of marketing can provide a fairly accurate picture of the resources used in different territories, or for different groups of customers or product lines, it is easy enough to establish input objectives for the next relevant period (quarter, half-year, or year). Against such inputs, it is also possible to forecast an output, so that input/output relationships reflect a considered view of the best use of resources. Objectives would, for example, be expressed not just in terms of required sales volume, but also in terms of required added profitability resulting from marketing activities. Advertising objectives might be expressed like this: "To raise the awareness level

Table 12.1 Basis of Allocation of Costs, Collected Under Natural Expense Headings

	Basis of Allocation		
Natural Expense Group	Territories	Customers	Products
1. *Order processing* Clerical labor costs Order processing and invoicing Telephone, postage Stationery	No. of orders	No. of orders or No. of items	No. of. orders/invoice lines for product
2. *Selling* Salary Commission Expenses Proportion of sales manager	Direct (SM ÷ by number of salesmen)	Cost per call x average no. of calls per year on customer group	Work study so as to apportion a salesman's time to selling each product
3. *Transport* Actual carriage costs Vehicle depreciation and expenses Insurance	Value of orders	Value of orders No. of items	Value of orders
4. *Reimbursement* (Allowance for bad debts) (Clerical costs for recovery)	Value of orders No. of orders	Value of orders No. of orders	Not allocated
5. *Stock* = amount of stock in warehouse x cost	Value of stock in warehouse servicing the territory	Not allocated (turnover rate)	Average value of stock per product Theoretical cost of working capital Space occupied by product in warehouse
6. *Stock control* Planning dept. staff	Not allocated	Not allocated	No. of inventory postings for product
7. *Advertising* Actual costs, specific to territory or product	Allocated by management	Only when it can be identified with a customer group	Only when it can be identified with a particular product

of potential buyers of Product X from 10 percent to 15 percent in the following year, within what would be the annual cost of eight salesmen," or "To double the recognition of package change benefits among present users of Product Y before the end of next year, within a cost level of $X."

Objectives for the sales force should also be expressed in precise terms. Achieving increased coverage, or obtaining best possible negotiated prices are, as seen in Chapter 6, too loose for satisfactory control of effectiveness. The output expected from sales costs in a territory might be expressed as: "To increase the coverage of chemical industry companies in the northeast by 25 percent by fiscal year-end." Or sales per product against product costs might be expressed as "An increase in revenue of 5 percent above forecast price levels for product line AB in the annual invoiced sales figures." Only in this way can the alternative usage of resources be judged.

Activities and "Payoff"

The final aspect of control of marketing activities is checking on whether activities happened and if they paid off. There is a great deal of inertia in most companies about existing arrangements. No one challenges the existing system of selling, advertising, or sales promotion. If things are not going well there is a temptation to look for solutions in trying to improve the quality of what is done, rather than questioning the basis—and then changing it.

Examination of activities must ask the questions: Did it happen? and Did it pay off? For instance, examination of the call rate should show whether the appropriate number of calls were actually made on customers. Everyone nowadays knows how to grade customer potential and relate it to call rate. But did the salesman's call rate meet the plan?

The question "Do we need salesmen anyway?" can only be answered if the payoff from direct salesman/buyer confrontation can be shown to be fruitful. It often cannot, and in those circumstances it is worth conducting a controlled experiment to establish the real results of the salesman's activity.

In one company, a total change in the calling pattern in a specific market demonstrated that the impact of the salesmen on the sales results, with their current method of calling and their way of approaching clients, was at best marginal. A cynic would assume from the results that salesmen's calls could be discontinued. As a result of the experiment the whole calling pattern was revamped, and the sales approach was completely rethought.

Another method of examining payoff is to take a critical look at what is actually happening in sales areas. Areas with equal potential and the same number of salesmen can produce different results for reasons such as concentration, experience of salesmen, ease of travel, which require examination.

Checking on a second area of marketing activity is equally divisible into "Did it happen?" and "Did it pay off?" Advertising and sales promotion activities should be checked to see if:

- They fit in with the marketing plan.
- The intended audience was aware of the advertising action. ("Have you seen this product advertised?").
- The coordination with the sales plan of sales promotion was achieved.

Measuring the effectiveness (the payoff) of advertising is fairly well documented in terms of research findings, but it is not so often used in practice. Managers still hide behind the remark that is attributed to a whole range of different captains of industry—"I know that 50 percent of my advertising budget is wasted; the problem is to discover *which* 50 percent."

The method is to isolate one item of the marketing mix—in this case advertising—from the others, and in a controlled experiment vary quantities and timing and assess the result. It is not difficult to do this by using the local radio station, local newspapers, or local TV, though the amount needed to make the experiment meaningful is often larger than might be thought.

Coverage and penetration as compared with competitors is a first step in checking activities in channels of distribution; buyer surveys, speed of throughput, and effectiveness of packaging and pricing are steps in examining the payoff.

The important part of control is to look not only at what has happened but at whether the result is justified in relation to the input—and once again to ask the question: Do we need more money in *this* activity or *that* activity because the result of this is better; i.e., how do the results of two more salesmen compare with another $150,000 in advertising?

Final Remarks

Control of the effectiveness of marketing is often neglected partly because of the belief that marketing is an exercise in creativity and partly because the tools are not available. This chapter has attempted to remedy both defects.

Today the drive is toward improving quality—an even more difficult task. The development of quality controls is an essential part of the marketing manager's function. Indeed a currently accepted definition of quality is "meeting customer requirements." Control mechanisms are thus not confined to the numerate aspects of marketing, but include the intangibles like customer satisfaction. The skill needed is the skill of being aware that *every* decision in the business must be made with a full knowledge of its impact on the customer.

Checklist for Chapter 12

1. What proportion of your total revenue is marketing cost? What proportion of the price paid by the user is swallowed up in marketing?
2. Are the uses of resources regularly examined and the results across the board compared?
3. Is there a "race-card" of controllable factors and a measure of input and output?
4. Can your accountant present marketing figures showing allocations by product, territory, or customer?
5. Have experiments ever been conducted to check the real payoff of salesmen, sales promotion, or advertising? What were the results?

APPENDIX

References

Chapter 1
1. Townsend, Robert. *Up the Organization.*
2. Drucker, Peter F. *The Practice of Management.* New York: HarperCollins Publications., Inc., 1986.
3. Ansoff, H. Igor. *Corporate Strategy.* New York: Pelican Books, 1968.

Chapter 3
1. Bonoma, Thomas V., and B.P. Shapiro. "Evaluating Market Segmentation Approaches." *Industrial Marketing Management 13* (1984): 257–268.
2. Day, George S. *Strategic Market Planning.* St. Paul, MN: West Publishing Co., 1984.

Chapter 7
1. Marvin, Philip. "Executive Time Management." American Management Association Survey Report, Cincinnati University.

Chapter 8
1. Harvey, Jerry. *The Abilene Paradox and Other Meditations on Management.* New York: Free Press, 1988.
2. Allen, Robert F., and Saul Pilnick. "The 'Shadow Organization' and Corporate Success: How Behavioral Norms Are Affecting Your Organization." *Organization Dynamics* (Oct. 1972).
3. Pfeiffer, J.W., and J.E. Jones, eds. *A Handbook of Structured Experiences for Human Relations Training.* Ten vols. San Diego, CA: Pfeiffer & Company, 1969–1985.
4. Follett, Mary Parker. "Creative Experience." *Longmans,* (1924).

5. Strauss, B.W., and F. Strauss. *New Ways to Better Meetings*. London: Tavistock Publications, 1964.

Chapter 9

1. Gowers, Sir Ernest. *The Complete Plain Words*. New York: Pelican Books, 1979.
2. Ibid.
3. Stewart, Rosemary. *The Reality of Management*. Eureka, CA: Pan Books, 1967.

Further Reading

Benfari, Robert. *Understanding Your Management Style: Beyond the Myers-Briggs Type Indicator*. New York: Lexington Books, 1991.

Block, Peter. *Stewardship: Choosing Service Over Self-Interest*. San Francisco: Berrett-Koehler Publishers, 1993.

Bonoma, Thomas V. *The Marketing Edge*. New York: Free Press, 1985.

Gabor, André. *Pricing: Concepts and Practices for Effective Marketing*. Brookfield, VT: Ashgate Publishing Co., 1977.

Harvey, Jerry B. *The Abilene Paradox and Other Meditations on Management*. New York: Free Press, 1988.

Levinson, Jay C. *Guerilla Marketing Attack: New Strategies, Tactics, and Weapons for Winning Big Profits*. Boston, MA: Houghton Mifflin Co., 1989.

McConkey, Dale D. *How to Manage by Results*. New York: AMACOM, 1983.

Stapleton, J. *How to Prepare a Marketing Plan*. Brookfield, VT: Ashgate Publishing Co., 1989.

Tjosvold, Dean. *Teamwork for Customers: Building Organizations That Take Pride in Serving*. San Francisco: Jossey-Bass Publishers, 1993.

Whiteley, Richard C. *The Customer Driven Company: Moving From Talk to Action*. New York: Addison-Wesley Publishing Co., Inc., 1991.

INDEX

A

Accounting:
  major principles in, 174
  objectives of, 174
Action plans, 112
Activities:
  executive, 97
  input or support, 97
  output or control, 97
Advertising costs, allocation of, 216
Algorithm, elimination, 53
Allen and Pilnick, 130
Ansoff, Igor:
  matrix, 8
  purpose of the business, views on, 3

B

Balance sheet, 174
Banks, High Street, (see High Street banks)
Benefit structure analysis, 46
Boston Consulting Group:
  product portfolio analysis, 48
Break-even:
  assumptions, 202
  calculations, 202
  chart, 203
  formula, 204
Budgeting, in the management process, 187
  Budget/Variance Report, 188
Business as an entity, principle, 174

C

Capital:
  employed in the business, 192
  investment in new products, 195–197
  return on, when employed, 182
  working, 192, 193, 200

Capital and revenue, distinction between, 175
Cash flow:
  analysis, 191
  discounted, 197
  forecast, 192, 193
  marketing manager's influence on, 193
Characteristics and motivations, matrix of, 43, 44
Checklists:
  factor analysis, 81–82
  footnote about, 11
  market standing, 12
  marketing effectiveness, 220
  marketing information, 36–37
  markets and products, 68–70
  objectives, 65
  organization, 99
  planning, 16–17
  reports, 155
Committees:
  as communications media, 160–161
  criticisms, 127
Communication:
  barriers to, 146–147
  general principles of, 145
  instruments, 160
  skills inventory, 164–170
  subjects of, 143
  written, 147
Company planning:
  constraints and limitations in, 9
  key areas in, 7
  means of measurement in, 8
Company purpose, defining of, 4, 144
Computer printouts, 35
Contribution:
  accounting, 178–180
  customers', 87

product, 87
per unit report, 179
Cost centers, 173–178
Cost of goods sold, computation of, 176
Costing:
absorption, 186
direct, 186
rate of return, 186
Costs:
marketing and selling, 178
opportunity, 200
Customer acceptance scale, 29

D

Day, Professor George S., Article in *Journal of Marketing* for April 1977, 48
DCF, (discounted cash flow), formula, 198
Decision making, information for, 22
Double-entry principle, 175
Drucker, Peter:
The Practice of Management, 7
Dupont Company, chart of ROI, 180

E

Elimination algorithm *(see* Algorithm, elimination)
Exponential smoothing, formula for, 58

F

Factors:
controllable, "race card" of, 220
noncontrollable, 54, 209
Films, use of in presentations, 159–160
Finance for Nonfinancial Executives, training courses in, 214
Financial statements, 173
Financial Tools for Marketing Administration by Letricia Gayle Rayburn, 200
Flipchart, advantages of, in presentations, 159

Follett, Mary Parker, 101, 135
Forecasts:
of project aspects 196
of revenue, 178
of sales, 52
Full-cost allocation, 177

G

Galbraith, J.K., "industrial technostructure," views on, 101
Going concern principle, 176
Gowers, Sir Ernest, *The Complete Plain Words*, author of, 149, 153
Group performance:
improvement of, 129–130, 134–135
influences on behavior of, 130
norms in, 132–134

H

High Street banks, market segments for, 45

I

Information, collection of:
competitive, 28
strategic, 26–27
usage, 27–28
Innovation, assistance in, 114
Input/output relationships:
in control, 219
in marketing costs, 215
Insight into Management Accounting, An by Professor John Sizer, 184
Interaction analysis, score sheet for groups, 137
Investigation, an investigative technique, 113–114

J

Job analysis, 107–108
Job results guide *(see* Management guide)

K

Key areas (see Company planning areas in)

L

Least squares projection:
 method of, 59
 trend in, 60–61
Letters, writing of, 148
Limiting factors, identification of, 204

M

Mail order business, 76
Majaro, Simon, 15
Management development, failures in, 104
Management guide, 107–112
Managerial chain, 162
Market assessment, 19, 24–26
Market segments, 20
Market segmentation:
 benefit, 42
 demographic, 41
 geodemographic profiling, 42
 geographic, 40
 psychographic, 41
 purpose of, 39
 types of, 40
Market standing:
 checklist for, 12
 key area of, 7
Marketing:
 allocation of funds in, 207
 control function in, 208
 cost analysis in, 214
 costs of, 207
 productivity audit, 208
Marketing activities, 96
Marketing concept, x
Marketing information:
 major areas of, 20
 technical aspects of, 21
Marketing information systems:
 data provided by, 36
 four main activities in, 35
 preliminary investigation for, 32
Marketing mix, ingredients of, 71
Marketing planning, schedule for annual, 14
Marketing research, questions before undertaking, 22–24
Matching principle in accounting, 177
Meetings, as communication media, 161
Models, management, ix
Motivation, 114
MAT, moving annual total, 66

N

Natural expense group, allocation of, 216
Needs, manager's, 106
Norms and group behavior (see Group performance)

O

Objectives:
 and Cato the elder, 3
 checklist of, 65
 definition of, 128
 dimensions of, 63
 focus on critical factors setting of, 10
Objectives input, 215
Opportunity cost, 200
Order processing, allocation of costs of, 216
Organization:
 customer-oriented, 98
 principles of, 89–91
 relationships in, 93
 systems of, 93, 96
 traditional pattern of, 98
 types of, 91
Organizing:
 matrix structure, 88
 process of, 86
Overhead activity, analysis of, 212

Overheads, allocated and apportioned, 179, 214

P

Ps, the four, 71–80, 209–212
Pareto's Law, 65, 67
Payback calculation, 199
"Payoff" of marketing activities, 217
Performance standards, 109
Personal salesmanship, factor in the marketing mix, 79
Pfeiffer & Company, *A Handbook of Structured Experiences for Human Relations Training*, 134
Place, as factor in the marketing mix, 79, 210
The Complete Plain Words by Sir Ernest Gowers (*see* Gowers, Sir Ernest)
Planning horizon, 197
Plans, data provided by the information system for, 36
Plumber, looking for burst pipes, 214
Practice of Management by Peter Drucker (*see* Drucker, Peter)
Present value method or discounted cash flow:
    calculations, table, 198
    formula for, 199
Presentations:
    layout of, 155
    preparation of, 156
    speaker's briefing for, 157
Price, as factor in the marketing mix, 75, 210
Pricing, marginal, 186
Product, as factor in the marketing mix, 74, 209, 213
Product evaluation (*see* Information, collection of)
Product life cycle, 12, 197
Product manager, responsibility for contribution, 87
Product/market strategy, 19
Product portfolio analysis:
    cash cows in, 49
    dogs in, 49
    stars in, 49
    wildcats in, 49
Profit and loss statement, 174, 175
Profit responsibilities of marketing managers, 173, 179
Profit centers, 173, 178
Profit-volume: chart, 203
    formula, 204
Project evaluation, 192–195
Projectors, film, overhead, slide, advantages of, 159
Promotion, factor in the marketing mix, 77, 210
Public libraries, as source of desk research, 24
Punctuation, Mark Twain on, 154
Purpose, company, 3

Q

Quantified regret, table of, 201
Questionnaires, answering untruthfully, 27

R

Ratios:
    financial, of importance to the marketing manager, 182
    primary, of turnover and profit, 180–184
Reality of Management by Rosemary Stewart, 162
Receivables, 192
Reimbursement costs, allocation of, 216
Reports:
    as communication media, 161
    fallacies about, 150
    industrial, 149–152
    layout and content of, 155
    skeleton of, 151
Research market:
    agencies for, 23
    questions to be asked in, 22–24
Revenue, definition of, 177
ROAM, return on assets managed, 182

ROI, return on investment:
    calculation, 181
    uses of, 180

S

Sales forecasting:
    checklist for, 62
    external environment in, 53
    internal environment in, 53–54
    methods of:
    arithmetical, 57–61
    brick-by-brick, 56
    executive opinion, 57
Satisfiers and dissatisfiers, 104
Segmentation, market (see Market segmentation)
Segmentation, *post hoc*, 41
Selling costs, allocation of, 216
Skill, *OED* definition of, xi
Slides, use of, in presentations, 159
Stock control costs, allocation of, 216
Stock costs, allocation of, 216
Strategy:
    differentiated, 47
    niche, 48
    undifferentiated, 47
Strauss, B.W. and Frances, *New Ways to Better Meetings*, 135

T

Time analysis:
    delegation as a result of, 123
    time control techniques following from, 124–125
Time log, 119–122
Time-series analysis, 59
Time use by managers, 118–119
Townsend, Robert, *Up the Organization*, 6
Trading cycle, 194
Transparencies for overhead projectors, 159
Transport costs, allocation of, 216
TV camera, market characteristics for, 44

Twain, Mark, on punctuation (see Punctuation)

U

Up the Organization by Robert Townsend (see Townsend, Robert)

V

VDUs (visual display units), 35
Videotapes in presentations, 159
Visual aids, types and usage patterns, 159–160

W

Work study, operating times formula, 57

Z

Z charts, 69